ROCK GARDEN PLANTS

ROCK GARDEN PLANTS

New Ways to Use Them Around Your Home

by

DORETTA KLABER

Illustrated by the Author

HENRY HOLT AND COMPANY • New York

84977-0119

Printed in the United States of America

To

E. H. K.
Joe
and
Susan

ACKNOWLEDGMENT

To *Popular Gardening* for use of some extracts of text and of some of the drawings that have appeared from time to time in their publication.

Some closely related material has appeared in the New York *Times* and Bulletins of the American Rock Garden Society, the American Primrose Society, and the Journal of the New York Botanical Garden.

CONTENTS

FOREWORD

This book is intended only as an introduction to the beautiful alpine and associate plants we can grow in our gardens. It is hoped the reader will be inspired to fare further along this fascinating road, as the author continues to do. Some of the plants described are well known, others are rarely grown. In many years of gardening I have tried thousands of plants. All those mentioned in this book have survived through the years. They frequently have faced neglect, fought off bitter cold and burning heat, and in most cases have come up smiling.

Bailey's *Hortus Second*, the latest revised edition of which was published in 1941, is in general the authority for nomenclature and pronunciation. Scientific names are written in italics. Following the more modern and preferred system, no capitals are used on specific names and the double i is dropped in the endings. I quote from the introduction to *Hortus Second:* "It is necessary to state again that fixity or rigidity in botanical nomenclature is unattainable."

The Latin names of plants have been used throughout the book, for these names are precise and universal. So many popular names are used interchangeably to the point of confusion that any serious gardener needs to know, and use, the Latin names. In the Descriptive List of Plants, where a second Latin name follows in parentheses it means that the plant was formerly known by that name. The common or popular name— if there is one—follows the Latin name, after which comes the family name, since it is of interest to know which plants are closely related. In pronunciation, the grave accent (`) denotes the long sound of the vowel, the acute (´) a shorter sound.

Part I

CLOUD HILL

I

A NEW APPROACH

Every now and then the debris of old thinking has to be cleared away. This idea applies especially to the uses that can be made of the wonderful small plants of mountain and meadow, waterside, woods and plain. Even now, many still believe that these plants should be grown only in rock gardens, contrived or natural, out of sight of the house, in secret spots that could imitate, to a degree, their natural habitat. This point of view is changing, and if you will clear your mind of all the taboos and dicta on the subject you will find that you can use these delightful plants with their gay colors, interesting forms, and decorative foliage close to your homes. No elaborate rock garden is necessary to make them happy. Whether you have a city lot or a bit of ground in the country, you can make appropriate use of these plants.

Should your land be naturally rocky, or have outcroppings of ledges, there can be no more attractive decoration than alpine plants. On the other hand, they will look equally at home around your doorway planting, as ground covers or bold accents. They will be happy in a terrace or wall. They will enhance the appearance of a flight of steps. Many can be used as edgings to borders of some larger flowers. They may peer over the rims of pools or outline paving or stepping stones. Their uses are as varied as their appearances. There are flat carpets of thyme or veronica, mounds of pinks or candytuft,

3

the sharp upthrust of iris spears, fluffy spires of astilbes and tiarellas—clumps, mats, and rosettes—gray or green—furry or smooth—each one different.

These plants are especially in harmony with new homes where the emphasis is on glass and indoor-outdoor relationship. In the changes of level around modern houses, banks have given way to walls or ledges of stone, broken by flights of steps. Courtyards and terraces, with their emphasis on leisure, cry aloud for intimate planting. To appreciate these small plants fully, you must see them nearby. They are the perfect answer to plantings close to the house. A glass wall or picture window demands something worth looking at. One could weep to see the myriad of big windows used to frame a lamp—because there is nothing else of interest to look at. What a greater pleasure it would be to step outdoors and watch the development of these plants through the seasons. There is always something of interest to see—from their spring burgeoning, through their exquisite blossoming, their fascinating ways of forming and disseminating seeds, their autumn colors, their usually attractive winter appearance.

It is indeed surprising that these plants, many of them alpines with a short growing season, will accommodate themselves to lowland gardens. Fortunately you don't have to duplicate their natural surroundings, for it would be an impossible feat. You do have to give them an approximation of their soil and moisture needs. No one goes up in the high Himalayas to manure the soil. The plants there live among grit and stone, fertilized by the humus of their own dead leaves. Because of the slope of the mountainside and of the rubble amid which they live there is perfect drainage, and no standing water to rot their foliage, which is often fluffy or flannelly. Water flooding down the mountain as ice melts carries small stones and grit, half burying the small plants. They thrive on it. If, in your warmer climate, you give them water, drainage, a modicum of nourishment in stony, gritty soil, and mulch them with more stone chips, they respond with their brightly colored flowers

4

and concise mats or mounds of beautiful foliage. Too rich or too heavy soil is their undoing. When the soil is too rich the plants grow tall and spread wide, losing much of their charm, and frequently go more to leaf than to flower. When it is too heavy, they are likely to rot. Plants from the plains adapt to similar culture, though drier summer conditions are called for. Plants of the woods want a soil rich in humus, while waterside plants naturally like moist conditions. Given good drainage, nearly all have remarkable powers of adaptation.

II

CLOUD HILL AND THE DOORYARD GARDEN

It is many years since I first became interested in mountain plants and their relatives from the lowlands. I began by reading everything I could find on the subject. I had been gardening for myself and others for a long time, and thought I knew the run of perennials that would grow in a great part of the United States. But the books on alpine and rock plants opened a new and fascinating world. I was enthralled and started to grow as many as I could from seed. It is by growing plants from seed that you get to know them best. Like children, they give you some worries, but these are far outweighed by the pleasures.

Wherever we lived I grew more and more of these flowers. Finally, we bought an old run-down farm in northeastern Pennsylvania and it is here that I have grown all the flowers listed and sketched in this book. Some of my experiences in growing them may help you, too.

In addition to a little four-room house there was a group of outbuildings called "messuage." The accent was on the mess, but the setting was all an alpine enthusiast could desire. Adjoining the house were blossoming apple trees. The entrance drive, close to the house, was halfway up a steep hill; the house itself was about 2 feet below the level of the drive. The ground rose beyond the drive, an open rocky hill, about 100 by 100 feet, with a backdrop of trees and shrubs. Following the drive past the barn we found a hill covered with pleasant woods.

When I say rocky hill, don't imagine little stones sticking up here and there. There were great masses of rock, some low, some shoulder or even head high, thrown up in the remote past by a great convulsion of nature. They were covered by moss and lichen although at the time we bought the farm many were hidden by high weeds. There was a tiny pool fed by a spring at the upper end of the space, near the highway. The handful of soil I picked up was a gardener's dream. We investigated the water supply (so important in the country) and found another spring up near the top of the property; this had been piped to feed into the house by gravity.

We added a living room with a large window and a screened porch in front of it, facing the open hill. As the direction happens to be west we planted a sycamore tree to shade the porch on hot summer days.

On the downslope from the driveway to the house we inserted ledges of stone on one side of the steps leading to the porch. On the other side, the change of level was handled by scooping out the soil and stones so that a slight slope for drainage led away from the house. Three feet in from the driveway a 2½-foot retaining wall was built to hold the soil, taking up the difference in level, and to house some of the alpines. The

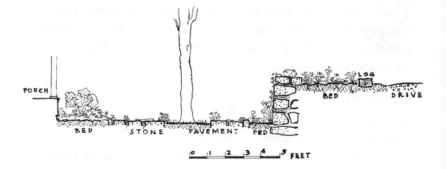

section shows how the wall rose a bit above the surface and the planting bed along the drive. A heavy oak timber rescued during the alteration of the house was used to edge the bed and protect it from traffic on the driveway side.

THE DOORYARD GARDEN

We see this little dooryard garden of wall, steps, and slope from the house and porch, and a step takes us into it. All parts get some sun but because of the sycamore, a nearby crabapple, and the west exposure, there is shade for part of each day. In our hot summers the plants welcome and thrive on it.

If this were the only space one had for a garden, it would be adequate. There is succession of bloom from early spring to heavy frost. All through the cold days of winter there are warm mats of evergreen or ever gray plants to greet you. There has been no conscious planting for succession of bloom, but a variety of flowers has been gradually brought in and planted for the pleasure of seeing their bloom, form, or foliage close by. Some positions are sunnier than others so it was possible to introduce plants with differing needs.

In summer the stones of the wall are almost hidden by dripping, hanging, spreading masses of flowering plants. Some of the choicest alpines are grown here, for drainage is perfect, and nowhere do they seem as contented as when they reach back with their roots into the cool depths of a wall. In winter some plants are dormant and disappear, others show a bud or a few green leaves at the surface. Those that stay seem to have added beauty—the encrusted saxifrages, for example. These sturdy plants that love the association of stones are attractive all year. The raised white edges of their leaves look like hoarfrost and in winter especially the edging stands out against the gray rocks.

This is a "dry" wall. I am frequently surprised by the misconception that many persons have as to what a dry wall is. It is a stone wall built without cement. It is not a wall built

9

only of stones. It should be laid up with the proper soil in the
joints and between the layers of stone, with wide joints here
and there for large plants. The purpose of the soil is to provide
the sort of home these plants like. The men who built the wall
for me were inexperienced and obstinate. I wanted them to
follow the directions I had read of sloping the wall backward,
and tilting the stones in it at an angle, so that water would run
into the bank and soil would not wash out. Now I'm rather
glad I didn't have my way. The wall stands firmly upright. In
most places the plants keep the soil from washing out. Occasionally I have to fill in some holes, but when I do, I try to put
in a rooted plant with soil so that it doesn't wash out again.
A small stone tucked under the root helps.

The flower show starts in earliest spring when *Eranthis
hyemalis,* the winter aconite, flings its gold at your feet, then
disappears for another year. *Anemone blanda* and hepaticas
show their blue and white or pinkish flowers soon after. Sweet
violets waft their odor to you before you realize they are out.
The early primroses (*Primula denticulata, farinosa,* and *frondosa*) have their stations at the foot of the wall, and there are
later primroses too. Androsaces are planted in abundance on
the slope, in the top of the wall, and in the bed beyond the
wall, for they particularly like the half shade and the very
gritty soil. In the same locations tiny drabas are among the first
to bloom, followed by the little townsendias and erigerons with
their attractive daisies. Pinks and columbines, creeping phlox,
iris and veronicas, candytuft and the "Persian candytuft,"
aethionema, are all represented by the smaller and rarer
members of their families.

There are some gentians for every season, spring, summer,
and fall; a few shrubby penstemons; the little *Arenaria rosea*
that blooms almost any time; as well as *Erica darleyensis,*
lavender cotton, saxifrages, and some of the finer sedums and
sempervivums for year-round decoration; potentillas, hypericums, geraniums, all low clinging plants with summer blooms;
midseason campanulas; delicate asperulas that would be lost

elsewhere; rare little shooting stars that here find conditions to their liking. Some of the tougher plants like *Scabiosa alpina* and double tunica give long summer bloom. Alpine forget-me-nots seed themselves everywhere.

There is room in this small area for plants of over 100 species. Auriculas (a kind of primula), which I could never make happy elsewhere in the garden, now are looking contented on a partially shaded slope at the end of the wall, with stones around their feet and a mulch of stone chips, while the slow-growing *Primula pubescens* hybrids are developing nicely at the foot of the wall.

There is a paved area in the 12-foot space between the narrow bed at the edge of the porch and the bed at the foot of the wall. Here the stones were set in sand over good stony soil that drains well, and many plants, placed either in the joints between the stones or in pockets of soil left for the purpose, have made themselves at home. Small paving stones were used to keep this area in scale and to carry out the informal appearance of the whole dooryard garden. Had our soil been impervious clay it would have been necessary to excavate deeper and to put a 6-inch layer of tamped cinders or other drainage material under a 4-inch layer of good soil and a 3-inch layer of sand above that before setting the paving stones and plants.

We have the advantage of having our house below the level of the driveway, so that the main part of the wall faces the house. If, on the other hand, a level terrace led from the house and then dropped to a lower level, as is more often the case, one could make a retaining wall to hold the terrace and then continue it as a double-walled parapet with soil between for a foot, two feet, or more above the terrace. This would give two exposures as well as the top of the wall in which to plant an infinite variety: either north and south, for sun and shade plants, or east and west, for alternating sun and shade. The double part of the wall would be built up with soil and some stones all the way through it. The top of the wall would be

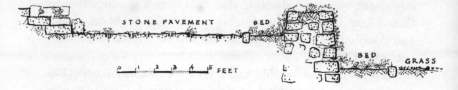

ideal for the smallest treasures, and also for plants that like to drip over the edge. Care must be taken to keep the hearty growers and the little ones separated, so the small plants are not crowded out. It is best to let the big ones fight it out among themselves and group the small ones near each other.

III

THE HILL

On the other side of the driveway is the rocky hillside. This could have been planted in any number of ways. It might have been turned into a heather garden (if the soil were right or made right), or a shrub garden or shrub rose garden (if you didn't want much work), or an iris garden, a garden of only native perennials, and so on—anything except a level lawn with borders! With this ideal spot to play with, what was more natural than to plant it as one large rock garden?

If, however, you do not have a rocky terrain but still want a rock garden, it is always possible to create one. It must be borne in mind, however, that the creation of a good, large rock garden requires great skill, often needing the services of a competent landscape architect or rock garden expert, and involving considerable expense. Too often, we see a bank with stones erupting like a bad case of measles, the mistaken notion of a rock garden. If you do the building yourself or supervise it, you must first have a clear picture in mind of what you want to do. Use as large stones as possible. Bury the greater part of each in the ground, putting its broadest side down. When it is placed you should be able to stand on the stone without dislodging it. Provide good drainage and a loose, gritty, not too nourishing soil.

Our hill is almost hidden from the highway by shrub roses planted along a wire fence. But from the porch and windows

13

we see and enjoy it winter and summer. How much people miss when they think of a garden as only a summer pleasure! In summer the flowery hill is framed in the green leaves of shrubs and trees. In winter it opens out to include the sky with its infinite variations of light and color.

Cedar trees, which are native here, have seeded them-selves here and there around the garden. A couple of goose-berry bushes were left for their warm winter color. A few other shrubs were added, each for some reason—winter or autumn color, midsummer flowers, or fruit. They also fulfill a second need, that of giving change of height to the garden and partially obstructing the view, so that as you walk around there is always a surprise to be found on the other side of a shrub or tree. A few taller perennials were planted. Because of the size of the rocks they fall into place naturally. For instance, yellow daylilies and purple Siberian iris give late spring color when the rush of early bloom is over.

The rest of the flowers are those usually listed as rock or alpine plants. They are a riot of color in spring, more subdued in summer, have much gaiety in the fall, and keep the ground clothed and warm-looking all winter. Most of them hold their foliage, and whether you look from the house or go out and examine them in detail, there is always something heart-warming to see.

Of course, we didn't just pull up the weeds on the hill and plant flowers. The hill poured water toward the house with every heavy rain. There were too many stones and too few planting areas. Paths and a sitting space were laid out; drainage ditches were dug along the fence and down the middle of the garden. This latter started at the natural pool near the road at the top of the garden, ran down a rill, and emptied into an artificial pool built under a vertical slab of rock, then emptied into the ditch. When there is plenty of water it goes singing down this little runway, tinkling over waterfalls and into a drain under the driveway, then on down. All paths are lower than planting areas. In emergencies, they act as additional drainage ditches.

Small rocks near the surface were dug out and used as edgings or for low retaining walls of terraces, the latter sloping only enough to avoid standing water. The soil was good and, because of the slope and the stony nature of the ground, it drained well. *Good drainage is the first and most important need for all alpine plants.* This cannot be overemphasized. To make doubly sure that the plants had what they needed, a

15

mixture of loose gritty soil was used to fill the beds. The proportions varied. What we aimed at was a friable soil, neither too sandy nor too stiff, with some nourishment in it.

Perhaps the most important ingredient is stone chips— ¼ inch to ½ inch. They keep the soil open and cool. They are also used as a mulch over the entire garden, discouraging slugs, keeping the necks of plants and foliage clean and free from standing water, protecting the roots from excessive cold and heat, helping to keep the weeds down, and giving a coherent natural look to the whole garden. In the fall an additional coating of stone chips is thrown around the plants as winter protection. Thus, we look out on a garden in winter, not on a mat of salt hay or evergreen branches. In early spring more prepared soil is spread over and shaken into all the plants to encourage sturdy growth.

WATERSIDE

Around the pools and along the rill are planted moisture-loving plants: primroses and gentians, trollius, forget-me-nots and astilbes, bluets and others. But if you have no pond or stream do not assume that you cannot grow moisture-loving plants. If you have a water supply and a hose you can. The behavior of the plants is somewhat different if the ground is naturally moist or if only kept so artificially. Take astilbe, for example. The big hybrid astilbes will be 2 to 2½ feet high when planted in a wet spot, with their great fluffy, colorful spires flowering in June and July. Planted in an ordinary border and receiving rainfall plus the hose they may be only 15 to 18 inches high, but still very attractive. In a small garden they may even be in better scale.

Scale is extremely important in any garden. Huge modern delphinium hybrids, for instance, are overpowering even among these large rocks. On the other hand, *Delphinium belladonna* is a species that in our gravelly soil grows only about 2½ feet high and looks in place.

16

IV

THE WOODS

Spring says "Primroses" here. From every half-shady spot in the garden primulas peek out. But the real primrose path is in the woods. This path is breath-taking in spring, when, among the huge boulders, primroses in every imaginable color bloom with other shade-loving flowers and ferns. Hepaticas rival the primulas with their earlier show. There are the phloxes (*Phlox divaricata* and *stolonifera*), narcissus, muscari, hardy cyclamen, irises (*Iris cristata, verna,* and *gracilipes*), dicentra, polemonium, anemones, precious little *Thalictrum kiusianum,* and many another lovely plant.

Where space permitted along the path larger planting areas were cleared. In the beginning, the path was not long, but as I grew more and more primroses and other plants from seed, divided the ones I had and added more flowering bulbs, the path, lined with blossoms, wound a hundred feet or so through the woods. Today the summer foliage of the undergrowth, left intact along the edge, completely encloses it and as one walks along the path one has the delightful sense of mystery found in places far from civilization.

The natural undergrowth in our woods is mostly benzoin, or spice-bush. We have left it wherever possible. It gives a quiet coherence to the woods and adds much beauty. Spring brings the glitter of its little golden flowers; summer, red or orange berries which the birds love; fall, an echo of spring with the golden leaves. If you have woods you want to use as a garden, by all means preserve the native undergrowth as much as possible. It provides a key to your plantings and makes the best possible background. Supposing it were laurel, azaleas, and blueberries. Then what fun to add the wonderful plants that would revel in the soil already there. Here would be the place for trailing arbutus, twinflower, shortia, and hundreds of other choice plants that like these conditions.

The preparation of such a woodland garden is not difficult. Stones are removed from pathway and planting beds, then used to edge the beds. Underbrush is partially cleared, any small trees in the way removed, bad weeds cleaned out. Any good native flowers or ferns that are not too invasive are left, or lifted and replanted. Then other flowering plants, little shrubby evergreens, bulbs, and ferns suitable to the soil are added.

If you haven't a natural woodland it doesn't take too long to invent one! Switchlike plants of crab-apples and cherries, dogwood and shadbush, inexpensive small plants of viburnums and other native shrubs, will in a few years grow into a bit of woodland, under which all the small plants can be naturalized. It is easiest to do this while your home is new, before grass and weeds take over. However, it is not too difficult to clear grass and weeds out of any space you want to use for the purpose. If there are already some big trees there it will add to the natural look.

TYPE OF SOIL

A garden-wise person will note that most of the plants mentioned in this book are happy either in a soil with a neutral reaction or in one on the limy side. The soil here has a natural limy reaction. By modifying with peat and leaf mold much of it is made neutral. Most of the plants needing an acid soil just don't like it here. It is possible to alter limy soil by the use of sulfur or specially mixed azalea soil but, except for a very few plants, I don't do this. Or you can remove whole areas of soil to a couple of feet in depth and fill in with the other type of soil.

My theory is that it is better to grow the plants that suit your natural conditions and will grow happily in them. One can't grow everything, so as long as primroses, gentians, and all the other lovely plants I list will grow with abandon here, why strive for "greener pastures"? Most heathers want a more acid soil than I have. A few heaths such as the *Erica carnea* group put up with my conditions, so I grow those.

Blueberries flourish in an acid soil, but with a peat-moss mulch or sometimes rotted sawdust, they grow and fruit well here. Gardeners who live among oaks and pines or hemlocks may have trouble adapting lime-loving plants to their soil. But what other riches they have to choose from! On the whole, most plants, especially if raised from seed, will adapt to your conditions. Another point: there are some related plants that like opposite soil conditions. Most of the Himalayan gentians don't like lime, though some of their hybrids do not object. The Japanese gentians seem to revel in a limy soil. I'm still trying to make the Himalayans happy here but, in the mean time, the Japanese and some of the European ones fill the garden with glory. I know I can't possibly live long enough to grow all the beautiful plants that would like it here, so, with only an occasional longing sigh, I tell myself not to be greedy and to enjoy the marvelous beauties that will respond with only reasonable care and no fussing or coddling.

V

BULBS, WILD FLOWERS, AND FERNS

Most field wild flowers, such as the common daisy, are too invasive to be considered here. The woodland wild flowers and ferns are, on the contrary, indispensable in any planting. Of the flowers, I have only discussed a few of my favorites. Space forbids a complete listing. There are many available, either from one's own property if one is fortunate enough to own a bit of woodland, from growers of native plants, or, in some instances collected from the wild to preserve them from bulldozers.

Of course, in spite of the above remarks, most of the plants considered in this book are wild flowers. Many are untouched-by-the-hand-of-man species native to alpine regions, some to prairie, arctic, or even desert habitat. Again, many of them have been hybridized. Primroses and gentians, for instance, while still of original species in many instances, have been crossed by plantsmen who have produced hybrids of outstanding quality.

There are books, too, about ferns; any open land or woodland has its species; catalogs list a wide assortment. Space forbids detailed discussion of them here, but no garden can do without at least some of them.

As for bulbs, I doubt there is a garden that does not have

at least a few. The list is long. There is a tendency, though, to omit many lovely species and concentrate on showy hybrids. The crocus is an example. The big crocuses that dot the lawns of the land are colorful and gay, but they are hybrids of dainty and beautiful species which are worth searching for. There are winter-, spring-, and fall-blooming species. Some to look for are *Cròcus imperàti, tomasiniànus, sièberi, biflòrus, chrysánthus,* and the autumn-blooming *speciòsus.*

Among the tulips (usually under the head of "Botanical Tulips" in catalogs) there are a number of species to be had, from the delicate candy-stick *Tulipa clusiàna* to the huge and showy *fosteriàna* Red Emperor.

Hyacinths, narcissus—each has daintier species than the hybrids with which we are more familiar. Hyacinths such as *Hyacínthus amethýstinus* and *azùreus* (*ciliàtus*) we rarely see listed, but most of the catalogs have the little narcissus species.

Cólchicums are autumn-flowering and look much like a large crocus. *Colchicum bornmùelleri,* blooming August-September with rosy-lilac cups, is considered one of the loveliest. There are many hybrids.

Sternbérgias, something like colchicums, provide the yellow the latter lack.

22

Lilies are legion. I like to see *Lílium pùmilum* (*tenui-fòlium*), a coral- or yellow-flowering 18-inch plant, as bright accents in the hillside garden. For moist positions, *canadénse,* with orange or yellow delicately formed flowers, is a beauty.

Bletílla is a hardy orchid with chunky tuberous roots that send up slender leaves and then lavender, typical orchid flowers on stems 12 to 16 inches high.

Chionodóxas are among the precious little bulbs. Most are starry blue with white centers but there are also pink and white ones.

Erythrònium, the dogs-tooth violets, or trout-lilies, are easy to establish but often hard to get to bloom. The yellow eastern species makes great masses of leaves in a moist spot, but the flowers are usually sparse. The far West is full of cream, purple, pink, and yellow species, some of which do fairly well in the East.

Fritillàrias have an odd beauty, many of them checkered in dull colors. The little yellow *Fritillaria pùdica* from our West is charming.

Galánthus, the snowdrop, with its early bloom, and the Leucòjum, or snowflake, larger and blooming in May, are both well-known.

Muscàri, grape-hyacinths, called bluebottles around here, are blue, white, or violet. They have an advantage in that they can be lifted in clumps with soil attached and moved at any time.

Puschkínia are less well-known little bulbs, with blue or white flowers.

The little Scíllas, or squills, blue and white in early spring, and the later *Scilla campanulàta,* blue, white, or pink are all invaluable.

There are a number I have omitted. Among them, some species of álliums, or onions, have lovely flowers but the leaves all smell like onions, so are not admitted here. Besides, I once tried one and found that they seeded around as prolifically as the wild pest we already have.

23

Brodiaèas and calochórtus, beautiful westerners, have not been hardy here. Orinthógalum, Star-of-Bethlehem, has nice white starry flowers, but what a fast-spreading weed!

It is fun and a great addition to our gardens to introduce a few new bulbs each year. Most need no coddling and provide welcome early color and are especially valuable because they will grow in the shade.

VI

PROPAGATION

The various ways of multiplying plants are described below.

GROWING PLANTS FROM SEEDS

Each winter I plant about 250 packets of seeds. For years I have been trying to find out which plants are hardy in this locality (northeastern Pennsylvania). Getting them up from seed has in most cases been no problem. With few exceptions, even the rarest and most difficult species will germinate generously. Getting them all to grow up is another matter. Many alpine species find our summers too hot for survival. Others don't like the soil. Of course, a few failures are not discouraging. I always try again to see if slightly different treatment will do the trick. But they are never pampered. Much as I would enjoy seeing the flowers, if they will not grow in the open with reasonable care, they are not for me. Here there is no alpine house and the coldframes I do have are only to get them started, not their permanent homes.

Each experienced gardener has his or her own way of growing plants from seed. The answer is that the one that works for you is the right way. New gardeners may, however, be scared off from the fun of growing their own plants from seed by the experts' talk of sterilization of the soil, the use of chemicals or refrigerator freezing, fluorescent lights, and so on. I therefore offer my easy methods with the word of caution

25

that I find them changing a little every year. My latest way is
as follows:

Seeds are ordered from tried and reliable growers. The
source of seeds is most important. Experienced growers go to
great trouble to sell seeds true to name and ready to grow.
On the other hand, seeds for the "tourist trade" or from care-
less suppliers may not come up at all, or if they do they may
not be true to name. Collected seeds of alpines are likely to
be true (though they may be natural hybrids) but they may
or may not be of the best varieties, for even in their natural
habitat there will be wide variation among individual plants.
Seeds from your own plants have the virtue of being fresh, but

again may be natural hybrids in your garden. (The term natural hybrid indicates cross-fertilization by insects, as opposed to hand-hybridizing as practiced by many growers.)

When seeds are received, from midsummer on, they are put in preserve jars with the rubber rings in place, the jars closed tightly and stored on a lower shelf in the refrigerator. There they stay until the first warmish windless days in January or February. (The wind could whip an expensive packet of rare seeds into space with one puff.) Then they are taken outdoors and planted in my homemade coldframes. These are far from tight—an advantage, since they never need the bothersome airing of commercial frames—and they are narrow enough to reach across without strain. The winter planting provides for the freezing and thawing and the cold period that many of the seeds need to germinate well.

The frames, with drainage material below the soil level, are prepared in the fall; that is, they are raked over and filled to within an inch of the top of the front board with the soil mixture I use:

1 part good loam (a wheelbarrow for measure).

1 part coarse sand or grit.

1 part stone chips, any kind, ¼ to ½ inch (put in for drainage and cool root run).

½ part peat moss which has been open to the weather and is not dry (it would soak up water needed by the seeds if used dry).

½ pail of spent mushroom soil or other very well rotted or dried manure or rich compost (the latter can be used in larger quantities).

½ cup of all-purpose powdered pesticide, to take care of any small creatures in the soil.

The same soil is then sifted over the surface to a depth of about ½ inch, and this in turn is just hidden by vermiculite, which helps to keep the seeds moist and seems to discourage weeds and bugs to some extent. Cell-O-glass (plastic-coated wire screening) covers are then placed over the frames, weighted down with stones. This keeps the prepared beds from being disturbed by animals or weather.

The seeds are planted in rows spaced 4 inches apart, no two close relatives adjacent, so that the species do not get mixed. Seeds are just sprinkled on the surface, patted in, barely covered with a light coating of sand (or not covered at all if you can't see them), watered with warm-to-the-hand water in a fine spray, and labeled. Newspaper, two layers thick, is placed over the seeds, and the Cell-O-glass replaced. The ground may be frozen underneath but the vermiculite will be soft to the touch, and of sufficient depth to press in the seeds. If there is snow on the ground the watering is omitted, the frame filled with snow and covered. After the snow melts you then give the seeds their dose of warm water and cover them with newspaper. Both the warm water and the icy cold snow help to soften hard seed coats, and promote germination; anyway, that's my theory. When it snows again more of it is piled into the frames.

In the bitter days of winter there is some heaving of the ground. One is always sure that all fine seeds, such as gentians, must be carried down too deeply, but it doesn't seem to work that way. The seeds seem to be raised with the heave and dropped with the thaw. Almost all come up in force eventually, and as they emerge another anchoring coat of sand is sprinkled on.

When the weather turns warm the glass covers are replaced by shade-cloth covers, a material made for the purpose, tacked to lightweight wood frames. This cloth has a very fine mesh that lets rain and sun go through but breaks the force of both. It is a great improvement over slat covers that allow rains to beat the ground into ridges.

In this cold season the ants and other bugs and slugs are not around and the seeds will probably sprout before they are molested, but as soon as there are any signs of animal life, Slugshot is dusted around and ant-traps placed about the frames. At the approach of mild weather the frames must be watched, watered as needed, for they should be kept moist, and at the first sign of sprouting the row is uncovered (one advantage of using newspaper, which can easily be torn off one row and left on others). At any sign of moss forming, or bugs under the paper, the paper is removed. At any sign of what appears to be wilting, that sudden drooping of seedlings, they are uncovered and watered with a mixture of 1 tablespoon of vinegar to a gallon of water. This simple remedy usually works. Transplanting the seedlings into fresh soil where they are not crowded may be advisable.

Some seeds sprout more readily in the dark, some in the light. In either case they usually come up. As soon as they are large enough to handle they are either separated and planted between the rows (if very small and fussy) or put directly into the nursery beds. The seedlings have to be lifted ever so carefully with an asparagus knife, kitchen fork, or other small tool. The soil in the frame is damp, so that they lift easily and can be shaken apart to plant each seedling separately.

With many it is important that their fine, and usually long roots be not broken nor allowed to dry out. I use an old pan or other waterproof container to lay the seedlings in, a row at a time. Should there be an interruption a little water can be put in the container to keep them moist until they can be planted. Otherwise they are transplanted quickly, as they are easier to handle if not too wet. It is good practice to handle the seedlings by their leaves, make a hole deep enough for the entire root system to drop in comfortably, then fill in, firm the soil, and water. As seedlings are removed from the bed some of the soil is naturally removed with them. The remainder is left in the beds, for long-dormant seeds may decide to sprout. Many an iris or other unpredictable seedling has come up long after the label has been lost!

PROPAGATION OTHER THAN BY SEEDS

Many people agree that seed-grown plants have greater

stamina and a longer life expectancy than those grown from cuttings, but if you want an exact replica of a plant, you must start with a cutting, layer, or division. Because of cross-fertilization, seedlings vary, which makes the use of seed interesting but also less reliable. You cannot always procure seed of some plant you just must have, while you may be able to secure the plant itself and propagate it in one way or another.

Plants from Cuttings.   For cuttings you need a sandbox. It can contain just sharp sand, or be mixed with an equal part of vermiculite, sifted sphagnum, or peat moss. A small coldframe or box with Cell-O-glass or polyethylene cover gives the close conditions they need, and a partially shaded position is advisable. The cuttings are taken from crisp new growth, not too young and not too old, the cut end dipped into a hormone rooting powder for insurance, though many will root without it. Some are made 2 to 3 inches long, cut just below a joint, the lower leaves removed. Others, like androsaces, are made from offset rosettes (which sprout out from the side of the plant), with a bit of stem left on them for an anchor. A ruler or other sharp-edged object is used to mark a row. The cuttings are placed about an inch apart in the sand, which has previously been moistened thoroughly and tamped. The sand is pressed tightly against them, watered again; kept damp but not too wet, until by signs of new growth you know the cuttings are rooted—or perhaps you lift one and take a peek when you become impatient. As soon as the roots are ¼ to ½ inch long I take the cuttings from the frame and put them into the nursery bed where they are left until they have developed a good root system and go into the garden. Of course, in the nursery they are watered and cultivated like the rest of the plants.

Plants from Layers.   A layer is made from a branch by cutting it halfway across on the underside, bending it down until the cut can be covered with earth, and holding it down with a stone, a hairpin or other method, depending on its size. After a few months you can lift the stone and if the branch has

30

rooted at the incision you cut it from the parent growth. You now have another plant. This is frequently done with many shrubs, such as *Cotoneaster horizontalis* and many of the shrubby alpines. With others of the latter all you have to do is cover part of the stem with soil and hold it down as above until it takes root. Androsaces, ericas, creeping phlox, are a few of the plants that lend themselves to this method.

Propagation by Division. Many plants can just be pulled apart, or heavy ones cut apart, and each division will make a new plant. Achilleas, for instance, root as they run, and can be pulled apart and each little rooted piece will make a new plant. Iris, with a few exceptions, can be lifted, have the soil shaken from the roots, the plants gently pulled apart or cut into pieces, each piece with some roots, foliage cut back half or more, and replanted. Most of the primroses respond to the same treatment, though cutting back should be less drastic. You will gradually find which plants benefit from division and which improve each year if left alone. A decrease in size of flowers or vigor of a plant is usually an indication that it needs division and fresh soil.

You will easily discover the suitable method of propagation. Aethionemas make one-stemmed shrubs—impossible to pull apart, so, use seeds or cuttings. *Androsace sarmentosa* makes a central rosette from which radiate stems which in turn produce rosettes at their ends, similar to the strawberry. Any plant with such growth can be layered or made into cuttings. Bulbs can be lifted at almost any time (but most safely when they are dormant), separated, and replanted or held dry until their normal planting period. Many of our western prairie flowers are dormant in summer and it is safer to divide them at that time. Some sort of marker is advisable so that you can find them!

HANDLING THE PLANTS

The main thing in cultivating or propagating plants is not to be afraid of them. If you decide some are in the wrong

31

place, or the colors are clashing, you can lift them, in or out of bloom, and move them to where you want them. The important thing is to dig the whole root system, disturbing the soil as little as possible, and move them quickly—soil and all—to their new position. Then, just as with the seedlings, you plant firmly, water, shade if necessary, and they hardly know they are moved. Watch them, and water as needed.

Any soil on the clay side tends to cake if handled when wet, and it may take years to get it back into a good growing condition. This is not the case with the loose soil mixture I use, and the only time I do not transplant is in winter or when there is a long dry spell in summer. Then, no amount of watering will take the place of a good soaking rain. The plants have all they can do to bear up under the heat and drought, just as you do, and they need all their strength to keep alive, let alone trying to re-establish themselves in new surroundings. On the other hand, when flowers are in full bloom in the spring they are at the height of their powers, the weather is usually favorable, and they can be moved with impunity. Fall, from mid-August to November, is another good transplanting season. I don't like to move plants much after November first, for they should be well rooted in before heavy frosts come to prevent being heaved out of the soil.

THE NURSERY BEDS

We chose a place for the nursery beds east of and adjacent to the barn. The barn gives afternoon shade and we have put a snow-fence roof over the area so the plants get some light morning shade. Here the seedlings are brought when they are big enough to move. What is "big enough"? Some say when the first true leaves appear . . . but only experience can tell the exact moment. There are some seedlings that resent too early disturbance, and if you have planted the seeds thinly enough they can stay where they are until they are sturdy young things. Others can be transplanted at any stage. If they come

32

up overcrowded it is safer to move them than to leave them to grow spindly, or perhaps damp off. One gradually learns the needs of each plant. They can't all be treated alike.

The nursery beds, edged with old bricks on end, are about 4 feet wide with 18-inch paths between, so that we can work from either side without strain. They are filled to within a couple of inches of the top of the bricks with the same gritty soil already described. The raising of the beds above the paths provides the needed drainage.

The old label is left in the coldframe in case some still dormant seeds decide to come up, and a new label placed in the nursery row. Here the tiny seedlings are spaced 2 to 6 inches apart, determined by their expected growth. A draba never needs more than an inch but a corydalis might want 6 inches. They are planted in rows about 4 inches apart to make for ease of cultivation. They now get cultivated and weeded about once a week—as soon as the ground is dry enough after a rain, to prevent too fast evaporation; or if it is too dry they are watered. At this stage they need careful watching; a day or two of neglect might prove fatal to some rare and difficult alpine. For remember: in their original homes they are used to melting snows seeping constantly among them, with the good drainage of the stony slope and gritty soil. The ground should be moist at all times but never have standing water. By early fall they are ready to move into the garden.

This may all sound difficult and complicated, but there are so many easy plants that keep you encouraged and hopeful while you struggle with some of the more difficult, and the triumph is so sweet when you succeed with those that test your skill, that you will surely keep on trying. Some, considered very difficult, will just like your soil and what you do for them, and when these plants respond happily to your care, what a joy that is!

A nursery bed has other uses than the care of young seedlings. Any collected or gift plants, or those sent from a distance, can be put there and watered and watched until they

33

have recovered. If you try to raise plants without this intermediate stage of the nursery and put your seedlings directly into the garden you will find (unless it's a very small garden indeed) that you forget to watch them—water them, cultivate them, and so on—and many will dry up or be overgrown by the larger plants around them, while if you nurse them along at first, they are eventually ready to take their places in the garden with equanimity.

Part II

THE PLANTS

Descriptive List of Plants

Achillèa Yarrow *Compositae* Composite Family

   A. ageratifòlia. This fine plant from Greece makes mounds of feathered gray leaves with heads of good white flowers with a whitish center, 6 to 8 inches high. The clumps increase grad-

ually and are readily divided. An even better plant is a variety known as *aizoón (Anthemis aizoon)* with entire, or uncut, leaves and larger flowers. The latter is particularly lovely in a wall, where it will bloom in May.

   A. clavénnae, from Europe, has silver-gray lobed leaves and increases its clumps slowly. Its heads of white flowers, much like *ageratifolia,* rise 6 inches, making it a pleasant plant to place among good neighbors. It is spring blooming.

   A. tomentòsa is the most familiar of the small yarrows and has a wide distribution. It is a slow creeper with heads of golden flowers 6 to 8 inches high, and soft, feathered gray woolly leaves (a wonder when the frost is on them!). For a light yellow, there is the form Moonlight, a most attractive plant with soft green leaves. Still tighter and more mosslike is *nàna,* with rather inconspicuous white flowers. The *tomentosa* group make fine ground covers; the hotter and sunnier the

location, the better they thrive. Evergreen and tough, they like poor ground. They are good in the joints of pavement and are not too invasive to use on wall or terrace or in the rock garden, where they will bloom from mid-May to mid-June.

Actinèa Actinea   *Compositae* Composite Family

    A. herbàcea is a sturdy American plant that deserves to be better known. It makes a 3-inch rosette of rough hairy leaves from which sprout 4-inch stems topped by deep yellow daisies,

each wedge-shaped petal having three teeth at the end. It needs sun and perfect drainage, blooms in spring, and can be propagated by either seed or division.

38

Aethionèma   Persian Candytuft   *Cruciferae*

Mustard Family

Aethionemas come from the Mediterranean region so a warm sunny position is indicated. At Cloud Hill they get an extra dose of stone chips around them as a winter mulch. Some of them may have part of the tops winterkilled but, if cut back to green wood in spring, they will soon branch out and delight you with their long season of spring bloom. When blooming is over cut the dead flower stems off to promote thick, shrubby growth.

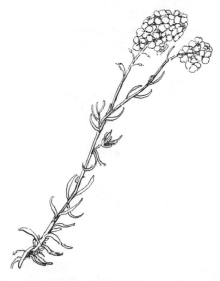

They are among the most delightful plants we can grow, shrublets of great charm. They are closely related to the candytufts, as the common name implies. However, we can easily tell the two groups apart. Most aethionemas are pink, while most iberis are white. Aethionemas have blue, silvery, or bluish-green foliage, while candytuft is usually deep glossy green. In addition, the flowers of iberis have uneven petals, two large and two small, while in aethionema the petals are all approximately the same size.

There are only slight differences between aethionemas:

A. *armènum, cordifòlium (Iberis jucunda), pulchéllum,*

39

schistòsum, and *stylòsum* all have bluish foliage and beautiful pale pink fragrant flowers.

A. *grandiflòrum* is often advertised but never appears. The nearest to it seems to be *theodòrum,* which is taller than the others (10 to 12 inches instead of 3 to 6), with rich deep pink flowers, somewhat larger than the others. It likes to get its roots under a stone and there is happy and permanent.

A. *iberídeum* is a white-flowered species with very small gray leaves.

A. *warleyénse,* a hybrid, has a quite different appearance from the others. The gray-green leaves are tightly pressed against the stems, giving it almost the look of a needle-leaved evergreen. The flower stems shoot out in all directions from the shrubby base and, though the individual flowers are small, they make up in quantity what they lack in size. The color is

a deeper pink than any of the others, the whole foot-wide, round, low shrub looking somewhat like a small *Dáphne cneòrum.* It blooms for weeks and, once well established, is a most valuable addition to the garden, though it lacks the fragrance that so enhances the others.

Ajùga Bugle-Weed   *Labiatae* Mint Family

A. *reptans* is a well-known ground cover for shade, which takes many forms, bronzy or green, 3 to 6 inches high, and comes in blue and purple, pink, and white. The leaves are practically evergreen and make quick-growing mats, surmounted by fine spikes of flowers. A. *genevénsis* is a nonspreading species.

40

Alýssum   Basket-of-Gold   *Cruciferae*   Mustard Family

The alyssums form a huge clan widely distributed over Europe and parts of Asia and Africa. They all prefer sun but will grow in part shade in light soil with good drainage and provide late spring and summer flowers.

A. alpéstre and the one often sold as *A. serpyllifòlium* are both prostrate plants with small rough gray leaves and clouds of small yellow flowers in summer. Use them in foreground planting.

A. argénteum can be used anywhere a small shrub is required. It grows 15 to 18 inches high with small rough gray leaves and good, rather flat, heads of little yellow flowers that bloom from late spring into summer. Occasional division keeps it within bounds.

A. idaèum comes from Crete. It is prostrate with silvery leaves rough to the touch and small flat heads of glowing soft yellow flowers. It is a lovely plant that should be placed so its drooping habit shows to advantage. Very close to *idaeum* are

species called *A. moellendorfiànum, scárdicum,* and *wulfeniànum*. All have similar growth but vary somewhat in size. All are attractive.

A. saxátile is the widely grown plant known as basket-of-gold. Its mound of large gray leaves over a woody base is surmounted by masses of brilliant yellow flowers in spring. Blooming with arabis and aubrieta it is the decoration of every rock garden. There are many forms. Variety *citrìnum* is a pleasing soft yellow, and there are double and compact forms

41

as well as hybrids of intermediate color such as Dudley Neville. A severe cutting back after blooming will keep it from getting leggy. Slugs have to be watched for under the heavy mats. It is best on a wall where it can have plenty of room, for it spreads wide with age.

A. *spinòsum.* This small plant from southern Europe is different from any of the others. It makes a woody, spiny, gray mound, 4 to 6 inches high, with small pink or white flowers. It is not as hardy as the others but is a pleasant plant for a protected position in sun.

Andrósace Rock-Jasmine   *Primulaceae* Primrose Family

These are precious alpine plants that no garden should be without. Some are very difficult to establish in lowland gardens but a few are most accommodating if you give them gritty soil with ample moisture, perfect drainage, and a mulch of stone chips. They are incomparable for walls and rocky banks in half shade.

A. *lanuginòsa* is a bit untidy in growth, making long runners from silvery rosettes and at intervals sending up a group of stems, some of which are topped by 6-inch high umbels of pink flowers, or white with contrasting eye, as in the form *leichtlíni.* It blooms in June. I do not find it quite so attractive as the following two.

A. *sarmentòsa* blooms in late April, two weeks after

A. *sempervivoides,* thus extending the season of these delightful plants. It starts with a woolly rosette and a flowering stem topped by a pink parasol, then sends out spokelike red runners that end in new rosettes. With a little help (a stone, a hairpin, or a landslide of soil) these will soon root and send out their own pink umbrellas and runners. They rapidly form pleasant colonies. Or the runners can be removed and planted as cuttings. There is great variation in size and woolliness of rosette and height of flowering stem, some growing 6 inches high. The variety *chúmbyi* is a particularly choice, compact form with rich pink flowers.

A. *sempervivoìdes* is not quite so easy as *sarmentosa* but is not to be classed as difficult. The rosettes are smooth, light

green, and arranged in geometrical form, decorative in themselves, and enhanced by their pink flowers. They are slower to increase than *sarmentosa* but use the same method.

A. *spinulífera* is more difficult. Its fuzzy rosettes, smaller than those of *sarmentosa,* throw no runners but gradually increase by adding new rosettes to the mat. Its deep pink flowers are lovely.

A. *villòsa* from Europe is really tiny. A good-sized rosette wouldn't cover a dime. Its half-inch stems are topped by white flowers. A silvery woolly morsel, quite hardy, but happiest if its wool is protected over winter by a small pane of glass. Of course, it needs a special spot where it won't be lost to view. It gradually adds new rosettes on very short runners.

Anemòne　　(Anémone)　Windflower　*Ranunculaceae*
　　　　　　　　　　　　　　　　　　　　Crowfoot Family

Anemones grow from a few inches high to a few feet. They all have more or less divided leaves, some lobed, some deeply

43

cut. There are a few difficult ones (A. *alpìna* and *vernàlis*) and many are uncertain from seed, which needs to be very fresh to germinate well. Once they are established they are hardy and delightful plants.

A. *apennìna* grows from a small tuber. It has large blue daisies, with narrow petals and, though not as attractive as the following species, it blooms a month later, thus extending the season.

A. *blánda* also grows from a small tuber. It is a native of Greece and can be bought from dealers in bulbs. Early spring brings up its lovely daisylike flower, 4 to 6 inches high, which can be blue, pink, purple, or white. After blooming the plant

disappears so it should be placed where it won't be disturbed. The half-shady edge of shrubs is suitable.

A. *canadénsis* is native to North America. It has good-sized white flowers on 12- to 15-inch stems and is supposed to spread rapidly. It has not done so in my woods where it is a pleasant addition without being outstanding.

A. *hupehénsis* is the Chinese version of the Japanese anemone. It is best in the woods or a shaded spot where its clean large pink flowers on 15- to 18-inch stems brighten up its corner. The three outside petals (really sepals) are a dark raspberry color, while the three inner ones are paler, a rich combination. It has the added virtue of blooming in late summer and fall. There is a beetle that likes to eat the leaves— and no leaves, no flowers—so it is advisable to spray early with arsenate of lead or other stomach poison.

44

A. *japónica.* Of course you will want this stately plant, if you have room for its 3- to 4-foot stems. It is a gorgeous beauty with white or pink, single or double flowers, which bloom in shade in late summer and fall.

A. *narcissiflòra,* from the mountains of the Old World, has special charm. It grows a foot high with inch-wide creamy-white flowers and firm dark-green cut leaves. It blooms for a long time in spring.

A. *pulsatílla.* This is the European Pasque-Flower, one of the most decorative of early spring plants. Its dissected woolly leaves are low on the ground when its large purple cup-shaped flowers with golden stamens bloom. The leaves lengthen as the flowers mature and turn into balls of fluffy seed heads. There are many hybrids covering a wide range of color in lavender, purple, pink, and white. The feathered seeds need to be planted fresh to germinate well and should have only a light sand covering.

A. *quinquefòlia* is the delicate little native wood anemone.

A. *sylvéstris* is a fine woodlander, about a foot high,

topped by one or two large white flowers. In cool or wet weather they are cupped (like the sketch) but spread wide open on a warm sunny day. It takes time to become established but when at home it will spread by underground runners.

Antennària Everlasting   *Compositae*   Composite Family

A. dioìca ròsea is a naturalized American. It makes a fine silky gray mat, then, in spring sends up its pink pussy-toes in pleasing contrast. Wonderful for pavement, wall, or any place in light soil in sun. A splendid ground cover, it roots as it runs

but can easily be controlled and can be pulled apart, each division with its bit of root making a new plant. Cutting off the flower stems after blooming keeps it neat and ornamental.

Aquilègia Columbine   *Ranunculaceae*   Crowfoot Family

Columbines are not only one of the important flower groups but are universally beloved. With a few exceptions they are easy to raise from seed. Seed of ordinary kinds can be broadcast in a shady place and will usually come up, but the alpines need careful planting—the kind described under Propagation (see Section VI). All have beautiful foliage, usually held well below the flowers. They grow in sun or part shade, some starting in early spring, others keeping on until early summer. The alpines need light soil and perfect drainage. All columbines hybridize freely, so you never know what may come up in your garden—which is fun.

A. akiténsis, from Japan, is a lovely little bushy plant

growing up to 6 inches, with blue or purplish flowers touched with pale yellow. It blooms for a long period in spring.

A. canadénsis is our wild spring columbine, which can be a 6-inch fairy growing in a crack of a rock, or a great 15- to 24-inch bush in good soil in sun. Its dainty red and yellow flowers hanging on delicate stems are beloved by both humans and hummingbirds.

A. chrysántha is one of our native long-spurred, tall species. Its soft yellow flowers have an exceptionally long season of bloom, carrying on from spring into summer, if not allowed to seed. It is one of the parents of the long-spurred hybrids.

A. clematiflòra, a tall hybrid, gets its name from an absence of spurs, making flowers open and flat. It comes in many colors.

A. ecalcaràta is a delicate-looking little thing from Japan, with a very low clump of lacy leaves and flowers of a dark

wine red. Its unusual cup-and-saucer blossoms need a background such as a white wall or gray rock to show off their odd beauty.

A. flabellàta, from Japan, is a great favorite with all who see it. The beautiful waxy flowers, either creamy white or light blue and white, are held just above the firm well-spaced leaves, which are bluish green with great appeal of their own. A dwarf form, *nàna,* is 6 inches high, the normal species 10 to 12 inches.

47

A. jònesi is a high alpine from our western mountains. It is a real miniature, much sought after, with little curled leaves close to the ground. Its flower is held just above the leaves, large for the size of the plant, but to my mind, lacking the beauty of form and color that many of the others have. This is a reddish purple with rather straight medium-length spurs, not quite fulfilling the promise of the lovely little leaves.

A. pyrenàica is one of the pure delights of late spring. Its lovely blue flowers with a brush of yellow stamens are held above the fine lacy foliage, which has a bluish cast. The whole plant is about 6 inches high.

A. scopulòrum, a choice native, is often spoken of as the loveliest of all. The very finely cut silvery foliage makes a 3-inch clump, while the blue, long-spurred flowers float above it on 6-inch stems. There are pink and lavender forms, sometimes listed as *perplexans*. It blooms in early summer.

A. viridiflòra comes from Siberia and is 6 to 8 inches high,

with odd brown and green, fragrant flowers. It is an interesting plant for a choice, well-drained position where its modest beauty can be seen.

There are many other beautiful columbines. One is the wonderful, long-spurred A. *caerùlea,* the Colorado state flower, but it is not long-lived with me.

Árabis Rock-Cress   *Cruciferae* Mustard Family

A. *álbida* is the well-known, rampant, mat-forming plant that sheets large areas with its gray woolly foliage and snowy expanse of flowers. The double form, most attractive, is reminiscent of double stocks on a smaller scale, but I have not found it as long-lived as the single-flowered type. There are good pale- and deep-pink forms but these vary greatly from seed.

A. *alpìna,* from the European mountains, is smaller, greener, and less rampant, thus making it a better associate for smaller plants. It also has white flowered and pink forms.

A. *aubretioìdes* is a compact plant from Asia Minor with purplish pink flowers and firmer leaves than that above. It will make a 4-inch mound.

Arctostáphylos Bearberry   *Ericaceae* Heath Family

A. *ùva-úrsi* is an evergreen shrubby creeper, a native, with white urn-shaped flowers and red berries. It is one of the

finest ground covers for dry, sunny places. It will cover acres of ground in open sandy soil as at the Waukegan Flats above Chicago and on Cape Cod, or it will grow slowly in partial shade in your own back yard. It prefers a soil on the acid side but will live in a limy soil made neutral by the addition of peat and sand. Its glossy leaves take on interesting tones in winter.

Arenària Sandwort   *Caryophyllaceae*   Pink Family
   A. laricifòlia is a delicate but showy little plant from

Switzerland. It sends out its 3-inch-high white flowers over a long period in spring.

   A. montàna comes from southwest Europe. It has rather straggly, sparse stems and small, gray-green pointed leaves, so that it is always a surprise to find it producing large and lovely white flowers. It is spoken of highly in most books on alpines and is beautiful when in bloom. Although it is supposed to be easy and rampant, I find it hard to keep. You might not. Plants behave differently for different people.

   A. vérna caespitòsa is found on both European and American mountains. Sometimes listed under *Sagìna* or *Alsìne*, it makes flat green or golden mossy mats, depending upon the variety, that look much like pincushions when the little white flowers are sticking in them. It is very good for use between

stepping or paving stones or just for green mats in half-shady, moist places. It is often spoken of as a sun lover but has a tendency to brown in spots in dry positions.

Armèria Thrift   *Plumbaginaceae* Leadwort Family
These are plants for sun and good drainage.

A. juniperifòlia (A. caespitòsa) is a high alpine from Spain with small, sessile, spiny-looking rosettes that produce pink or white chaffy flower clusters close upon them. It is a miniature to be placed among other little treasures. A mulch of stone chips keeps it clean and an occasional top dressing of gritty soil encourages the slow growth.

A. marítima grows up to 12 inches high but is usually represented in gardens by its form *laucheàna* that makes clumps of short grass above which, on 4-inch stems, the bright rose flowers bloom for a long period in mid-spring. Frequent

top-dressing is advisable. If the clumps begin to look ragged, division is wise. The tufts can be separated and, if any are without roots, a period in the sand bed will remedy this. They are splendid plants where a low edging is wanted, or they will make a bright spot in a pavement.

A. plantagínea is sometimes offered under the name *A. formòsa* or Formosa Hybrid. It makes clumps of broad leaves, 4 to 6 inches high, then 18-inch to 2-foot bare stems are surmounted by globular heads of typical thrift flowers in various shades of pink. This is a background plant and careful staking will keep it from falling over in a storm. Good staking is always practically invisible. The mistake of using stakes longer than necessary is frequently made. If the stake above ground is ⅛ the height of the plant and the tying loop is made firm but not too tight, stems will remain upright but will not look stiff. Another error in staking is to try to tie too many stems to one stake. This always looks awkward. One of the good qualities about most of the plants named in this book is that they require little or no staking.

Artemísia Wormwood   *Compositae* Composite Family
A. *dracúnculus* is the European herb tarragon, the leaves of which are used in salads, stews, and to flavor vinegar. This makes an 18-inch bush with narrow, pungent-smelling leaves. The flowers, if they bloom at all, are inconspicuous. The plants are readily divided.
A. *frígida* is from the prairies and thrives in sun and poor soil. Its low mounds of cut leaves are frosted silver and of sufficient beauty to be independent of their inconspicuous yellow flowers. I always cut the flowers off to keep the clump compact and attractive.

Asclèpias Butterfly-Weed   *Asclepiadaceae*
Milkweed Family
A. *tuberòsa* is one of our native roadside plants still seen in summer and early fall. Its brilliant reddish-orange flowers do, indeed, attract the butterflies. Its midsummer bloom comes at the same time as sweet lavender and they are good companions. The butterfly-weed grows 2 feet high and can be used as an accent in the garden. It is hard to transplant except when young, because it makes a long tap root. Grow it from seed.

Aspérula Woodruff   *Rubiaceae* Madder Family
A. *hírta,* from the Pyrenees, has the typical square stem, whorled leaves, and tubular flowers of the group but it is on such a small scale that one just sees a furry 2-inch mat sprinkled with tiny pink-budded, white flowers with four pointed petals. It is a pleasing plant that spreads slowly and must not be overgrown by its neighbors. There are some choice pink-flowered asperulas if you can (1) get their seed and (2) bring them up to flowering size. Like so many alpines the seedlings are temperamental but, once the plant is mature and placed in a suitable position, it is perfectly hardy at our lower altitudes.

52

Áster   Starwort   *Compositae*   Composite Family

There are countless native asters and still others from many parts of the world. They are spring-, summer-, or fall-blooming.

A. alpìnus is the spring-blooming aster from the mountains of the world. It grows 3 to 10 inches high with hairy basal leaves and fine large daisies in pink, blue, or white.

Plant collectors seem to have had a special liking for it, for there are three closely related species named after their discoverers: *A. fárreri, púrdomi* and *forrésti.* The last has very narrow rays. *Purdomi* is 6 inches high, while *forresti* is a foot high with a bright orange disk in the center. These species were all found in Tibet and China. They are all sturdy perennials, easily divided, and add much beauty to the spring scene, blooming in rotation after the first rush of flowers.

A. kúmleini is a Midwestern native that is most welcome for its late bloom that starts in August and keeps on for a long time. It comes in good pinks and blues and its clouds of small daisies are most effective. It grows 12 to 15 inches tall, is sometimes erect but more often droops. It spreads by underground stems but is not a nuisance and is a good solution for holding banks in poor soil in sun.

The fall asters have many low hybrids. In addition to the round mounds of named varieties, there are low creeping mats being developed, called Blue Carpet, etc. And, of course, for borders, the tall Michaelmas daisies, developed from our road-

53

side asters, are well known and provide handsome and varied color.

Astilbe Astilbe   *Saxifragaceae* Saxifrage Family

This is a most valuable group of plants for late summer bloom, preferably in shade, though if kept moist enough they can be grown in the sun. The big hybrid astilbes derived from Japanese and Chinese species come in many named varieties ranging from white through good pinks to red. They are lovely at the waterside or anywhere they can be kept moist. They grow 2 to 2½ feet high and bloom in midsummer. The clumps increase fairly rapidly, forming a hard crown. They can be divided by a spade, leaving some roots on each division. There are a number of dwarf varieties; all are delightful and flower even later than the big ones.

A. *chinénsis pùmila* grows 6 to 8 inches high. It has a soldierly appearance with straight, upstanding flower stems. The deeply cut leaves make low mats that increase by under-

ground runners that send up clumps of leaves at their ends. Naturally, they divide easily. The flowers open from pink buds from the bottom of the spike upward. The lower flowers with fluffy stamens, lavender tipped, form little bottle brushes while the upper ones are still in bud.

A. simplicifòlia, delicate-looking, is really very hardy. It also grows 6 to 8 inches high with glossy, entire, pointed-lobed, and toothed leaves as well as airy sprays of little cream or pink flowers. There are a number of forms with slight differences of color and height. The clumps increase and can be divided by careful pulling apart. A peaty or woodland soil suits it best. Nothing could be lovelier for late color in shade.

To gather the excessively fine seeds of these small astilbes one must wait until the flowering stem and spray are brown and dry. Then pick the whole stem and store in an envelope until the dustlike seeds drop out. The stems can then be removed and the seeds stored in the refrigerator, as described under Propagation (see Section VI), until planting time.

Aubrièta Aubrieta   *Cruciferae* Mustard Family
Originally from Europe and Asia Minor and formerly spelled aubrietia, the aubrieta hybrids have long since pushed the species out of commerce. Their foliage looks something like arabis but is a darker gray and not quite as large. They are suited to sun or part shade, where they will make gradually increasing mats of bright spring color ranging from pinks through reds and lavenders to purples. They do best on a bank or on the top of a wall, where they get perfect drainage, but

they should not be starved. It is wise to select them in bloom if you don't grow your plants from seed, because some can be harsh in color. They can also be propagated by cuttings, by detaching some of the long stems in September and rooting them in the sand bed. A heavy top-dressing of soil several times during the season keeps them bushy and floriferous and a good shearing back after blooming encourages neat growth.

Auricula—see *Primula*.

Bèllis English Daisy   *Compositae* Composite Family
B. rotundifòlia. This little 3-inch white daisy and its

lavender variety *caeruléscens* come from Algeria and vicinity. They increase a bit in size with age and the pleasing flowers start in May and keep on for a long time. In well-drained gritty soil they live over winter and even self-seed where happy.

Béllium Bellium   *Compositae* Composite Family

   B. minùtum, from Europe, is an even more charming daisyling. The rosette of spoon-shaped leaves is barely 2 inches across. The bright white daisies with pink striped under sides (which makes the buds look pink) are about 2 inches high.

They are enchanting, showy, and where free from competition will creep slowly around. They start blooming in July from winter-sown seed and keep on blooming for a long time in sun or half shade (where they do best) if not too dry. They are good plants between paving stones where they won't be stepped on.

Brunnèra Forget-me-not Anchusa   *Boraginaceae*
Borage Family

   B. macrophýlla *(Anchùsa myosotidiflòra)* is a Siberian plant. The heart-shaped leaves are small when the deep blue, foot-high, airy forget-me-nots bloom in spring. As the flowers fade the leaves enlarge until we get big masses of rough, dull-finished, large leaves. They do best in partial shade where they make a fine accent. They should not be placed too conspicuously for they are deciduous.

Calceolària Slipperwort   *Scrophulariaceae*
Figwort Family

   C. biflòra, from Chile, is hardy here. It should be called the baby-slipper, for anything looking more as though it had just been slipped off a tiny foot would be hard to imagine.

The 3-inch plant with its one or two soft yellow flowers hanging above the slightly hairy leaves is entrancing. It likes a cool, half-shaded position with its roots under a stone and here withstands a winter or two.

Callìrhoë Poppy-Mallow   *Malvaceae*   Mallow Family
   C. involucràta, a native, likes a loose gritty soil in the sun. A good position for it is at the top of a high wall or bank where its long streamers can hang down 4 to 6 feet and make a bright spot all summer.

It has translucent crimson-silk blossoms with white centers. The flowers are an inch or two in diameter. The carroty roots of the young plants may be heaved out by frost but can be pushed in when the ground softens. They grow into great turnips as the plants age. In congenial soil the plants seed themselves prolifically and need watching; once established, they need a spade and a strong arm to get them out.

Callùna Heather   *Ericaceae* Heath Family

These come from Europe and Asia Minor. The heath family is a choice one, evergreen, floriferous, and with flowers on one or another sort throughout the year. If you have the

space and the acid soil they like, or can contrive it, nothing could be lovelier than a heather garden. They grow from mats to 3 feet high, and can be had in white, various shades of pink, purple, and red.

C. vulgàris. All the callunas are descended from this one species. In spite of their predilection for acid conditions, I have grown a few here by adding plenty of peat and sand to their soil. They are inclined to be winterkilled at the ends of the branches or, at best, they turn brown. A spring shearing brings them back and they revive and give their welcome late flowers from August on. Another cutting back after blooming keeps them compact; they improve with age. They are native to open ground and sun but there their thick mats must shade the soil and keep it cool. With me they burn up in full sun but will grow where they have half shade. See also *Erica.*

Campánula Bellflower   *Campanulaceae* Bluebell Family

This is a huge group and one of the indispensables, for most of the species start blooming in late spring or early summer when the rush of early bloom in the garden is over.

C. carpática comes from eastern Europe. It is one of the most commonly grown and has many forms and hybrids. Its big cups of white, lavender, or purple bloom in late summer. A very fine form is *turbinàta* with large flat flowers close upon its low mass of leaves. All the good campanulas are the favorite food of slugs, so it is wise to keep the neighborhood dusted with Slugshot, Snarol, or similar material.

C. cochlearifòlia (*C. pusílla*) is a European mountaineer. The low leafy little plants ramble around pleasantly and in late June bring forth a myriad of small hanging bells in lavender or white. Wherever you put them they are a delight—along

the walk, in chinks of steps, on top of a wall. The form Miranda is a bit larger in all its parts and even succeeds in improving on the type. Sometimes sold as *C. bellárdi*.

C. collìna, from the Caucasus, has strong clumps of 1-inch, scalloped, more or less hairy leaves on short stems. The flowering stems rise 6 to 12 inches with one-sided racemes of fine purple bells.

C. elatìnes and its close relatives from southern Europe are among the loveliest of all. Placed in the face of a wall it makes a central rosette of glossy-toothed pointed leaves from

60

which, in June, radiate sprays of white-centered, lavender stars.
A very special favorite of slugs. *Elatinoìdes* is a variety, very
fine but not quite as outstanding as *C. elatines* itself. It has
more upright growth and woollier leaves, though most campanulas seem to vary in this quality. *Gargánica*, long considered a species, is also a variety of *C. elatines*. From a packet
of seed you may get woolly or smooth-leaved plants with
toothed or deeply cut leaves. The flowers are starry in outline
and vary from white to many shades of lavender and purple,
some white-eyed. The mats or mounds of leaves are low with
the flowers held above them. Light shade and a well-drained
soil with ample moisture suit them.

    C. glomeràta acaùlis, from Europe and Asia, grows about
5 inches high and has deep purple flowers in dense clusters.
It is a bit stiff, only gradually increasing its clumps, but it gives
effective color in late spring.

    C. párryi (C. planiflòra), from our West, has great dis-
tinction. It is one of the most strikingly beautiful of the bell-
flowers. It has hard, dark green, cast-iron rosettes about 2

61

inches wide, and 4- to 9-inch stems with the large shallow cups of white or lavender bloom welded close upon them. It also flowers for a long time if fading flowers are snipped off. It starts in June but may show a few flowers for a month or two. It can be divided.

C. *persicifòlia*, from Europe, is the peach-leaved bell-flower, a 2- to 3-foot beauty with white or lavender shallow cups set closely up the stem. If the terminal ones are cut off as they fade, lateral blooming branches prolong its bloom. June.

C. portenschlagiàna (C. muràlis), from Dalmatia, for some reason has never gotten established here. It has bell-shaped flowers with roundish, toothed leaves and is one of the most popular in the family.

C. poscharskyàna, from Serbia, blooms from June on with great mats of firm leaves and big upfacing bells. It should not be put too near choice little plants. It does best in part shade.

C. rotundifòlia, the harebell or bluebell of Scotland, is also native over much of this country. Its name comes from its rounded basal leaves. Those on the stem are narrow and about an inch long. *Rotundifolia* is a very variable plant. Plants may be 6 to 15 inches high. There are innumerable forms and these change under cultivation. Like the wild columbine, it may be the daintiest of plants, clinging in a crack of a rock but in richer surroundings it will form a big bushy plant. Still, it is one we can't do without. It starts to bloom in June and, if dead flowers are occasionally cut off, will keep on until stopped by frost. It seeds around but is never in the way.

Célsia Celsia   *Scrophulariaceae*   Figwort Family

C. acaùlis is a lovely spring-blooming plant from Crete. The descriptions I had read of celsia being much like mullein didn't prepare me for the thrill I had when my plants first came into bloom. The neat rosettes of roughish leaves held

promise but the brilliant yellow flowers close upon them, emphasized by their brush of orange stamens, are breath-taking. They have a delicate fragrance, too. They are fleeting

but the buds assure continued bloom. It flowers the first year
from seed if planted early.

Cerástium Snow-in-Summer *Caryophyllaceae*
Pink Family
  C. tomentòsum. This well-known gray matting plant
comes from Europe. It is a terrific ramper, so must be placed
accordingly—for instance, to hold a rough bank in sun where
its showy flowers will be most effective. It blooms in mid-
spring and a heavy haircut after blooming will help to keep
it within bounds. It can be readily divided and also seeds
around so that seedlings have to be watched for and either
transplanted or pulled out.

Ceratostigma Plumbago *Plumbaginaceae*
Leadwort Family
  C. plumbaginoìdes (Plumbàgo larpéntae) is a Chinese
plant widely grown as a ground cover in sun or part shade.
It creeps underground and sends up 6-inch stems with glossy
leaves. In late summer it produces sprays of deep pure blue

flowers, a wonderful color rivaled only by the gentians, some
of which bloom at the same time. It has fine autumn color, too.
It appreciates a good loamy soil and is readily divided.

Chrysógonum Golden-Star *Compositae*
Composite Family
  C. virginiànum. This sturdy native plant makes a rosette
of rather coarse, toothed leaves, about 3 inches long, and

64

quickly increases its clumps. It has starry yellow flowers and an exceptionally long blooming season, starting in late spring. It will grow 3 inches high in sun, taller in shade, and is invaluable where a colorful, no-trouble plant is wanted. It pulls apart easily, each rooted division making a new plant.

Chrysópsis Golden Aster   *Compositae*
Composite Family

C. villòsa, one of our western prairie flowers, has narrow, hairy, gray leaves and forms a bushy plant 12 to 15 inches high, covered with fine-rayed yellow daisies in summer. Another, lower form of this appears by itself in my garden. They are a pleasing addition to the summer bloom.

Convallària Lily-of-the-Valley   *Liliaceae* Lily Family

C. majàlis. Because of its heavenly odor no garden should be without the lily-of-the-valley. However, it should be kept on the outskirts where its invasive ways will not cause trouble. Its fragrance will pervade the garden, nevertheless. It is always spoken of as a ground cover for shade but I have seen it blooming more prolifically in sun. It won't stand too much drying out.

Coreópsis Tickseed   *Compositae* Composite Family

C. auriculàta is a native. It can be either slightly woolly or smooth. It has low tufts of leaves and branches. It spreads by runners so that it soon makes a large patch. The orange flowers, about 6 inches high, resemble the big border coreopsis but are deeper in color and not quite so large. If the withered

65

blooms are kept cut, it will bloom from late spring into summer. It divides easily into rooted pieces.

C. ròsea, also an American, is quite a different plant. It grows about a foot high, has very fine leaves and pretty pink daisies. It is perennial though not a permanent inhabitant like *C. auriculata.*

Corýdalis Corydalis *Fumariaceae* Fumitory Family

C. lùtea, from southern Europe, grows about a foot high with the most delicate airy-looking leaves and racemes of pale greenish-yellow flowers. It is at home in part shade and woodland soil and is worth growing for its foliage alone. Brittle stemmed, it must be placed where it won't be disturbed and where, if pleased, it will seed itself.

C. sempérvirens. I have this under the name of Alaskan corydalis. It is a charming biennial, 6 to 12 inches high, that seeds itself in gritty moist soil, so that once you have it, you rarely lose it. Its basal leaves, blue with pink stems, are beautifully cut and make a graceful fountain, exquisite when sparkling with dew. It is an astonishingly beautiful plant that hardly needs the pretty pink, yellow-tipped flowers.

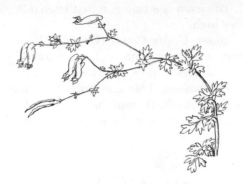

Crássula Crassula   *Crassulaeceae*   Orpine Family

    C. milfòrdiae, from Basutoland is hardy. It makes very small rosettes that turn red in winter and has little white flowers on inch-high pink stems, conspicuous in spite of their

tiny size. It can be pulled apart like a sedum and each piece replanted. It creeps slowly, so it can be safely put among choice little plants.

Cýclamen Cyclamen   *Primulaceae*   Primrose Family

    These are natives of Europe with cormlike roots, small hardy versions of the florists' cyclamen. All appreciate woodland soil and part shade. The corms should be planted near the surface with not more than 2 inches of soil over them. I found it difficult, at first, to tell top from bottom. The roots come out around the sides and even the flowers sprout from the side of the top. The smooth side of the corm is the *bottom.* It is most discouraging to find an old corm, 3 to 4 inches wide, which has made a plant a foot wide, neatly eaten out by the squirrels. Poison dusted around and some sharp bits of tin stuck into the ground near them seems to help.

C. cilícicum is a tiny one that enchants me—only a couple of inches high.

C. còum. Under Coum Hybrids I have had some spring-blooming cyclamen with lightly marked green leaves and flowers in shades of pink on 3-inch stems.

C. europaèum. This one adds fragrance to its other attractions. Its marbled, roundish leaves of an inch or two in width, are glossy, very decorative, and almost evergreen.

(All cyclamen have a dormant period when the leaves disappear.) Its deep rose flowers appear in late summer and keep on for quite a while.

C. neapolitànum comes in pink or white with red spots at the base of the flower. I have seen this one naturalized in the woods under a mat of ivy, which no doubt discourages the squirrels and protects self-sown seedlings over winter. The corms make great mats of leaves and flower for a long time in the fall. The leaves are dormant when the flowers first appear but soon come up and keep on enlarging until they may be 3 inches long on 3-inch stems. They are handsomely marbled and patterned and persist all winter.

Cyclamen can be grown from seed, taking several years to reach blooming size. They need protection from heaving in winter in their early stages. This, aside from buying corms, is the only means of increasing your planting, as the corms make no offsets, merely increasing in size each year.

Cymbalària   Kenilworth Ivy   *Scrophulariaceae*

Figwort Family

C. muràlis (Linària cymbalària), a delicate little European vine, is a charming addition to a wall where it roots as it runs and can be easily thinned out if it gets in the way. Its little mauve snapdragons blossom pertly here and there most of the

time among their cool-looking, light green leaves. It is hardy in spite of its frail appearance.

Delphinium Larkspur   *Ranunculaceae* Crowfoot Family
In addition to the gorgeous matronly hybrids, there are many species of delphinium. Few are really long-lived perennials but all are a pleasant addition to the garden.
D. belladónna and *bellamòsum* are really the light blue and dark blue forms of *D. cheilánthum formòsum*, which comes from Siberia and China. In poor soil in sun they will not exceed 2½ feet. In rich soil they grow 3 or 4 feet high. Their clear blues add much to the June garden.
D. bicolor, from our western mountains, is a fine plant 8 to 10 inches high, with dark blue flowers touched with dull yellow. It persists for several years in a well-drained position in sun or light shade and blooms for a long period in spring.
D. grandiflòrum *(D. chinénse)* is the 15- to 18-inch Chinese larkspur, with feathery leaves and rich blue flowers, used in borders.
D. nudicaùle, a Californian, looks more like an odd columbine than a delphinium. Only 8 to 10 inches high, it has

69

blossoms of a warm coral touched with yellow, or yellow flowers. It does best in light shade.

D. tatsienénse is a little 6- to 8-inch plant with fine blue flowers, needing careful placing to show its delicate beauty.

Diánthus Pinks   *Caryophyllaceae*   Pink Family

This is a beloved group. There are many species and innumerable hybrids, large and small, single and double. One of their many virtues is that most carry their good gray or green foliage over winter. After their late spring bloom is over a good shearing will keep the mats neat and usually promote a second crop of flowers in August when they are more welcome than ever. They thrive upon frequent top-dressings of soil. Most come readily from seed.

D. alpìnus, from Europe, is among the most beautiful, though lacking the fragrance that endears so many of them. The mats of dark, glossy, firm leaves produce big, pink-speckled, toothed cartwheels. It varies in height from 1 to 4

inches and is long-lived if given a partly shaded position or one where its roots are cool and moist, yet protected by good drainage.

D. arenàrius, from Finland and Dalmatia, likes a sandy soil in sun or light shade and there will mold itself to rocks or bank in a flat mass of short fine grass which in June will be covered with 3- to 4-inch frothy, fringy, sweet-smelling little flowers in white or pink.

D. barbàtus. Sweet William will always have a place. Its dwarf forms have their uses but lack some of the old-time charm of the taller varieties. Given a semiwild position they seed and renew themselves.

D. deltoìdes, the maiden pink of England, makes flat mats and will make a lawn of small green glossy leaves, hidden when in bloom by a forest of 6-inch-high small flowers of white to dark red, some with speckled zones. It is an excellent ground cover where it can be given room and holds its foliage over winter.

D. glaciàlis, from Europe, makes small round greenish-gray tufts close upon which sit round pinks with toothed edges.

It has neither the size of *D. alpinus* nor the rich warm pink of *neglectus* but in its own right is a pleasant little thing. Like all these small pinks it wants a gritty soil, sufficiently moist, in sun or part shade.

D. gratianopolitànus is the name now given to old *D. caèsius,* the lovely cheddar pink of England and the Continent. Sweet-smelling, it makes 6- to 8-inch mounds of blue-gray foliage covered with flowers of soft pink. There are attractive doubles and beautiful related little forms or hybrids two of which are called *D. arvernénsis* and La Bourbrille.

D. negléctus, a European mountaineer, is a favorite. It has very fine short grass of a grayish green without the midrib that *D. glacialis* has and then either has flowers close upon it or else the stems are 3 to 4 inches high. The taller ones may be labeled *ròysi.* The color is an especially warm, rich pink with a bluish eye and a buff reverse. This coloring is constant and is a sure sign of whether you have the true species or not. It is said to be lime-hating but is not fussy here and is long-lived in well-drained positions in the rather poor soil it likes.

D. nítidus, another European, has small tufts of green, glossy leaves. The good pink flowers, with dark calyxes bloom on 6-inch stems in early spring, the first of the pinks in my garden.

D. noeànus (Acanthophýllum spinòsum) is still another one from Europe. It makes hard mounds of thick, short, gray-green grass, sharp to the touch. Its flowers are fringy, white, and small on 6-inch branching stems, not showy, but oh, the fragrance!

D. plumàrius is the Scotch pink. Its big blue-gray mounds and foot-high, large, fragrant, fringy or toothed flowers are well known and much beloved. It has been hybridized extensively. It is long-lived and will seed around unless given a severe haircut after blooming, in June.

Dicéntra   Bleeding-Heart. Dutchmans-Breeches
Fumariaceae   Fumitory Family

D. cucullària. The lacy leaves of Dutchmans-Breeches and the hanging white, yellow-tipped flowers, about 6 inches

high, are found in shade in rich woodland soil, usually in the
cracks of rocks. It will grow and spread in similar positions in
our gardens but does not always consent to bloom.

D. *exímia* from the East and *formòsa* from the West are
two good summer-blooming bleeding-hearts for half-shade.
Both have ferny bluish-green foliage, pink hanging "hearts,"
and grow about a foot high. They hybridize freely and vary

in size, in leaf, and in color of flowers. *Eximia* is the larger and
spreads faster. "Sweetheart" is a popular-named white form of
formosa, while *eximia* also has a white form that opens pale
pink.

D. *spectábilis* is the big old-fashioned bleeding-heart from
Japan, making 2- to 3-foot bushes. It is hardy everywhere, and
though usually used in gardens can be grown appropriately at
the edge of woods. The leaves disappear in midsummer so it
should be placed with this in mind.

Many other lovely dicentras can be grown, including *D.*
oregàna, a low silvery plant with white, purple-tipped flowers.

Digitàlis Foxglove   *Scrophulariaceae* Figwort Family
The tall foxglove of woods and border is biennial but
there are also a number of perennial species.

D. *ambígua,* from Europe and Asia, has 6-inch leaves in
tufts and sends up 18-inch to 2½-foot stems of pale yellow

73

flowers in spires in June, when they are most welcome. It prefers half-shade and divides readily.

D. dùbia, a lovely plant from Spain, grows less than a foot high with soft pink "gloves" and woolly leaves.

Dodecàtheon Shooting-Star *Primulaceae*

Primrose Family

These are all beautiful natives, lovers of partial shade and moisture in their growing season. Hillside or wall planting for the small ones gives them the good drainage they need. They disappear completely after blooming but reappear as surely

74

in the spring if not disturbed. They can be grown from seed but the leaves of the seedlings also disappear, leaving a tiny bud atop a few roots. Knowing this, one acts accordingly. They may also be divided after blooming when the crowns have increased enough to pull apart into divisions.

D. amethystìnum has clumps of light green leaves about 4 inches high, purplish flowers and pointed stamens and petals streaming backward, a delight to behold. It blooms in early spring, 6 to 8 inches high. When you have pictured one shooting star you have described all of them, except for variations

in size, color of leaves, and flowers. *D. radicàtum, tetrándrum,* and *vulgàre (pauciflòrum)* are all close to *amethystinum* but with even more attractive coloring and pinker tones.

D. mèadia is a larger plant growing to 12 inches or more, with pinkish, purplish, or white flowers.

Dorónicum   Leopards-Bane   *Compositae*

Composite Family

D. caucásicum. From rather large basal toothed leaves rise 15-inch stems with good yellow daisies early in spring. A smaller, daintier version with finer-rayed flowers of a deeper yellow is *cordifòlium.*

Dràba   Draba   *Cruciferae*   Mustard Family

Drabas, from many lands, are among the earliest flowers to bloom. They can hardly wait for spring and a warm winter

75

day will sometimes open the little yellow or, more rarely, white flowers. They can be divided roughly into two groups, one that has spiny rosettes, each leaf eyelashed at the edges, and the other with softer leaves, minus the hairy edges. Sometimes one needs a magnifying glass to determine to which group a plant belongs! Sun and good drainage amid other small companions are indicated.

D. aizoìdes with its green rosettes and yellow flowers is typical of the first group. Others in this class are *dedeàna,* a lovely white one with large flowers over soft gray mats; *D. háynaldi,* yellow; *olýmpica,* light gray-green mats that send up ample heads of good yellow flowers on 1- or 2-inch stems and look like a small alyssum; *rígida,* a stiff yellow-flowered one; and *rupéstris,* white.

Of the second group *D. mollíssima* makes tiny soft gray rosettes but has never withstood the winter here. A little larger and sturdier is *polýtricha,* with delightful gray rosettes, yellow flowers close upon them.

D. sibírica (D. rèpens) is different from either group. It has tiny green leaves on runners and small yellow flowers on 3-inch stems. It is a miniature ground cover to plant with other tiny plants such as *Armeria casepitosa, Androsace villosa, Dianthus microlepsis,* among many others.

Dracocéphalum Dragonhead   *Labiatae* Mint Family
D. grandiflòrum, from Siberia, is indeed a splendid flower. Eight to 12 inches high, it blooms in late spring and early summer with rich blue spiky heads of hooded flowers.

D. nùtans, from Central Asia, is about 6 inches high with pleasantly scalloped rough leaves and earlier spikes of blue-purple flowers. It looks so much like ajuga that it is frequently mistaken for it, though the foliage is different. Though not as attractive a plant as *D. grandiflorum,* it is more persistently perennial.

Edraiánthus Edraianthus   *Campanulaceae*

Bluebell Family

These come from Italy, the Balkans, and thereabouts. There are only botanical differences between *Edraianthus* and *Wahlenbergia* so, if you are looking for one, be sure to look under both headings. Farrer divided them according to whether they have single flowers on each stem or clustered flowers. The botanists make it harder for us and now most of the well-known species are grouped under *Edraianthus* but catalogs still list some under the other. In any case, they are a very attractive group, very close to the campanulas, and have lavender to purple upfacing flowers on short stems amid tufts of grassy foliage.

E. dalmáticus, graminifòlius, kitaibèli, and *tenuifòlius* are cluster-heads, summer-blooming, while *pumílio* and *serpyllifòlius* are single-flowered. *Pumilio,* in addition, has finer, grayer foliage than the others, and where happy will cover its silvery leaves with a mass of lavender flowers in late spring. All must have well-drained locations in gritty soil, are happy in a wall, slope, or ledge, and must not be placed where heartier growers would smother them.

Epimèdium Barrenwort   *Berberidaceae* Barberry Family

These come from the north temperate zone. They are lovely ground covers for woodlands or other partly shaded areas. They are closely related to the *Vancouvèrias* of our West Coast. They vary in size from 6 to 15 inches and are white, yellow, red, or violet. There is great confusion in their naming. They have differences in form, and many are hybrids. Those most generally found in cultivation are *E. grandiflorum (E. macranthum),* its varieties, and hybrids known under the names of *E. versicolor* and *E. youngianum.* The delicate foliage of all epimediums, carried gracefully on wiry stems, would be sufficient reason for growing them.

E. grandiflòrum differs from the plant pictured in having larger flowers with long spurs on the inner petals, giving them

77

the appearance of an odd columbine. The flowers rise above the leaves and each flowering stem has a single, three-parted leaf.

E. versícolor sulphùreum is the one most commonly met with—yellow, but otherwise rather similar to the one pictured.

E. youngiànum ròseum is crimson and white, but the color varies. The leaves are edged in crimson, adding to their

decorative quality. Variety *níveum* is a low plant, 4 to 6 inches high, with pure white flowers. It increases more slowly than the others.

Eránthis Winter Aconite   *Ranunculaceae*

Crowfoot Family

E. hyemàlis. The first warm days in late winter and early spring bring out the 3-inch-high golden buttercups of the

little European winter aconite. The round yellow buds with their Elizabethan ruffs show up before the divided leaves. A warm day will open the flowers but when it turns cold again they close up and wait unharmed for better weather. The plants spread rapidly, both by increase of their tubers and by seeding. Plant them, then, in congenial soil in a woodland or some half-shady spot where they can remain undisturbed. They disappear like most bulbous plants after ripening their seeds.

Erìca Heath   *Ericaceae* Heath Family

These come from Europe and South Africa.

E. *darleyénsis* is a hybrid that has proved hardy here and not averse to my soil. I grow it in a sandy, peaty mixture in half shade. Full sun is usually recommended but mine do better in part shade. It has rich, pink, urn-shaped flowers that start blooming in late winter and keep on for a month or two. The needlelike leaves are evergreen, making a most satisfactory little shrub of a foot or more. The branches can be layered readily.

For a heather garden, as mentioned under *calluna*, many of these heaths should be included. *E. cárnea* is the winter-flowering heath. It has many varieties. *E. cinèria* is the bell heather, a summer-bloomer. *E. tetràlix* is the Cornish heath, a summer- and fall-bloomer. So, with the summer- and fall-blooming callunas, plus others of the heath family, one can have all-season bloom from this group alone—in addition to their usually evergreen foliage.

Erigeron Fleabane   *Compositae* Composite Family

These are very close relatives of the asters as well as the townsendias, varying from both in having more crowded ray flowers. They come in all sizes, many of the taller ones being rather weedy, with flowers small in proportion to the size of the plant. However, some of the small ones are most attractive. All of the following are American alpines.

E. aùreus is an adorable miniature. At Cloud Hill it sits on a wall with small clumps of spoon-shaped leaves, while close upon them appear the little solid looking golden daisies. The whole plant is under two inches. It is best in lime free soil and must have a carefully chosen, well drained position.

E. compósitus has gray, finely dissected leaves in low mounds and is covered with small white daisies. It is among

the first plants to bloom in spring, flowers intermittently all summer, and may be among the last to bloom in fall. It is absolutely perennial.

E. símplex (*Townséndia formòsa*). A tuft of grayish-green,

slightly hairy leaves an inch or two high. Lavender daisies on 3-inch stems emerge from a hairy bud that keeps a petticoat of fluff under the flowers. It always surprises me by being so hardy and persistent.

E. ursìnus grows about 6 inches high with one-inch-wide lavender flowers that bloom all spring and summer.

Erìnus Erinus   *Scrophulariaceae* Figwort Family
E. alpìnus, from the mountains of Europe, is a most attractive little plant. Once established, it is persistent, seeding itself here and there in well-drained corners, hugging a rock,

or otherwise protecting itself from the elements. The first year it is likely to be only an inch or two high but it then grows taller. It comes in red and various shades of purple, has some named varieties, and can be grown from seed or divided.

Eròdium Heronsbill   *Geraniaceae* Geranium Family
Very closely related to the true geraniums, these are much desired. (The florist's so-called geranium is a *Pelargònium.*) Most of the good perennial species have low clumps of attractive, dissected leaves, with white, pink, purplish, or striped flowers and the fascinating heronsbill seed heads. It is difficult to procure the seeds or plants of many of them.

E. chamaedryoìdes ròseum comes from the Balearic Islands. It makes the nicest little flat clumps of wavy-margined

81

leaves on 1-inch stems. The flowers are pink with red veins. It is a choice morsel for a partly shaded, moist, well-drained spot.

E. manescàvi, from the Pyrenees, sometimes acts biennial but usually seeds around so that once you have it, you really have it. Its green dissected leaves take on red tones in the fall.

The flowers, purplish pink on 6- to 8-inch stems, start blooming in midsummer and keep on the rest of the season. Planted near the blending geranium colors or near white flowers, its color is enhanced.

Gentiàna Gentian   *Gentianaceae* Gentian Family

The gentian family is a huge one. The members vary from being easy, to difficult, to almost impossible to grow. There are spring-, summer-, and fall-blooming plants. There are creeping, low, and tall species. There are some whites, and a few yellows, but most gentians are famous for their blues— light blue, deep blue, robin's-egg blue, purple, and gentian blue. They are among the most interesting and beautiful plants we can have in our gardens.

All want ample moisture and good drainage. Most want part shade but there are many sturdy ones indifferent to sun

82

if they have sufficient moisture. I have tried every kind of gentian of which I could get seed. Practically all have come up, many have bloomed, some were not true to name, and others were not of sufficient interest or beauty to continue growing. They hybridize freely, and one may get forms or varieties from seed.

I find it easiest to classify gentians into spring-, summer-, and fall-blooming kinds. The main ones in spring are the *acaulis* and *verna* groups; in summer, *septemfida* and *decumbens;* and in fall, the gorgeous Himalayan and Japanese species. Although the list is alphabetical for convenience, the group to which each member belongs is indicated.

G. acaùlis, from Europe, is a big-flowered, spring gentian of the Alps, and is considered a group of closely related species, including *angustifòlia* and *kochiàna*. Their character-istics are large stemless trumpets close upon firm, usually glossy, evergreen leaves, arranged in first-year plants in a

Greek-cross pattern. As the plants increase, this definitely symmetrical form is lost. The flowers are huge for the size of the plant, great upfacing trumpets of rich blue, spotted inside, usually with a white throat. There are five petals with folds between. In the *acaulis* group these are almost as large as the petals. Other gentians may have nicks or fringes between the petals while some omit them entirely. *G. acaulis* itself is difficult. It comes readily from seed, is perfectly hardy, and multiplies its rosettes each year, but doesn't care much about blooming. No one seems to know the answer to this. A rich soil in sun or half shade is recommended and then it will do all or nothing for you. Some forms are more reliable about blooming, but most seem to wait two years from seed.

G. álgida (G. romanzovi), from our West, is a dwarf plant

83

with large trumpets of a disappointing washed-out white; I found it not worth growing.

G. *ándrewsi* is the native closed or bottle gentian. A well-grown plant will reach 18 inches and, covered with dark blue, budlike flowers, it is very attractive. It is best suited to a semi-wild position at the edge of woods. It blooms in late summer and fall.

G. *asclepiadèa,* a southern European, known as the willow gentian, is too tall for any but background planting, and it prefers half-shade. Its great 3- to 4-foot stems of blue or white trumpets are showy and add good summer color.

G. *bisetaèa* is a good American, summer-blooming, similar to *septemfida*. Its 12-inch reddish stems end in single trumpets of blue.

G. *cachemírica* blooms in late summer. It is a crevice plant with small silvery-green leaves and delicate, upfacing, wide-open trumpets of clear blue, marked with purple and yellow. It is difficult to get the true species but one should keep trying. Its lovely flowers bloom in late summer and fall.

G. *calycòsa* comes from our West. It blooms in summer, grows about 8 to 10 inches high, has heart-shaped leaves, and flower petals widely separated by the nicked folds between them.

G. *crinìta* is the beloved fringed gentian. It grows 12 to 24 inches high. Because of its four-petaled, large, four-angled flowers, and wild fringiness, plus its clear soft blue color, there are not many gentians that surpass it in beauty. However, it is only a biennial, found in wet meadows, usually in the sun, in late summer and fall. It can be grown from its very fine seeds if handled with care. Sifted sphagnum moss surfacing the bed will prevent the damping off that sometimes afflicts it. The seedlings are best carried over the winter in a protected coldframe or coldhouse, as they are still tiny at the coming of frost. Planted out in a suitable place in the second spring, they should bloom that year. If really at home, it might reseed itself and so become established.

G. *cruciàta,* from Europe and Asia, makes glossy, leafy 8-inch plants, then tops them with clusters of 4-petaled flowers too small for the plant, though when well grown the quantity of deep blue flowers has something to say for itself. It is absolutely hardy and permanent and blooms in July. There are a number of other hardy, upright summer gentians but all are of secondary value.

G. decúmbens. This is taken as the type of a group, most of which are Himalayans but not *the* Himalayans that one speaks of with bated breath. *Decumbens* makes a central rosette of glossy, 4- to 8-inch-long, vertically veined leaves.

Long stems spray out in spokelike fashion from this hub and end in bunches of small blue bells, which vary from light blue to dark purple. A raised position shows them off to advantage. Any good soil suits them so long as you remember to supply copious water and good drainage. They have a long midsummer season, sending out additional clusters of lower flowers as the terminal ones fade. A well-grown plant is wonderfully attractive.

G. fárreri is typical of *the* Himalayans, with their marvelous color and mass of bloom in late summer and fall. At first sight the leaves of *farreri* are disappointing—so straggly, thin, grasslike. However, when the robin's-egg blue, 2-inch-long trumpets appear, you can see why all the to-do. It is difficult to get true *farreri,* but if you can, and it has the right soil (they all prefer soil on the acid side), they increase by stolons,

making big mats covered by ice-blue flowers adorned with exterior striping, a truly amazing sight.

They all need stony, sandy, peaty, cool soil in partial shade, near water if possible. In any case, they must be kept moist, and a heavy top-dressing of gravel or stone chips will aid in this. After years of struggling to meet their needs in my rather limy soil, I am succeeding at last, with light and dark trumpets opening in their sandy, peaty, slightly sloping bed at the edge of the woods where they get sun for a short time in the morning and are open to the air. They live over winter in this position with no mulch other than the stone chips.

G. freyniàna is one of the *septemfida* group. They are more concise than the latter, about 6 inches in all directions. The good blue flowers are usually borne singly on the stem.

G. gracílipes is one of the daintiest of the *decumbens* group but not as hardy as some. It has smaller, narrower leaves and shorter flower stems.

G. héxa-fárreri is a hybrid. It has the blue flowers of

farreri but variable, and its leaves are more like *hexaphylla*. It starts blooming in July.

G. hexaphýlla, as the name indicates, has its leaves and petals in sixes, giving it a particularly interesting, rich look. The leaves are shorter and broader than most of its close relatives. The flowers are rather squat and tubby, making it a most appealing plant. This is one of the Himalayans.

G. ínverleith is a gorgeous hybrid between *farreri* and *ornata.* The trumpets, which may be light or very dark gentian blue, are large and beautiful. It blooms for a long time, starting in August, and new buds form as the flowers fade. The foliage is somewhat stronger than that of *farreri.*

G. lagodechiàna is, more accurately, a *septemfida* variety with single flowers.

G. lùtea comes from Europe and Asia Minor. I once grew it and imagine it would still be with me if I had not pulled it out. I waited three years for the huge leaves to produce their flowers and when they finally sent up 3- to 4-foot stems with spires of a sad straw color I decided they had used up good space in my garden long enough.

G. olivièri (*G. dahùrica*) is another of the *decumbens* persuasion but not as good as some.

G. ornàta is one of the good Himalayans. It has charming tubby bells, blue with a white throat, and foliage less grassy than *farreri.*

G. phlogifòlia is a poor midsummer cluster-head from eastern Europe.

G. saponària is an American woodland species with narrow flowers barely opening at the tip.

G. saxòsa is from New Zealand and, like so many New Zealand flowers, is white. It is a small plant with dark, glossy, little leaves and bell-like flowers. The seedlings did not live over the winter with me but it is a lovely species if you live where it can be grown.

G. scàbra, from Japan, sets the type for an amazing group.

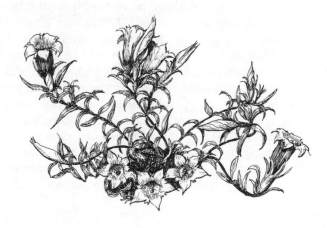

I have its variety *búergeri* in several forms: Kirishima, Tukasa, and Kumagawa Rindo (*rindo* is Japanese for gentian). Kirishima is *G. scabra saxátilis*. Its stems spray along the ground. From the tip of every stem and from every leaf joint very short stems emit single, upfacing, delicately formed flowers—a mass of deep blue. Tukasa grows 3 to 4 inches high; at each leaf joint there is a bunch of flowers instead of a single one as in Kirishima. These two bloom in September with 75 to 100 flowers on a plant. The effect is breath-taking.

Kumagawa waits till October. It is a larger plant with larger flowers. The outside is a glossy mahogany, so that you get red buds and some of the red showing through the flowers,

giving an iridescent effect. As the season advances the leaves turn dark red too. The flowers are a soft blue, contrasting well with the leaves. It, too, blooms prolifically.

It is best to place all the *scabras* where they get sun for most of the day, though midday protection from the hottest sun is advisable if you can arrange it. Either very close planting or a ground cover to keep the roots cool is advisable. They close their blossoms, like barometers, in cold or wet weather. This sometimes frustrating habit prolongs their bloom and the late ones keep on until hard frost. They disappear completely over winter but come up again in late spring. Because of their late bloom, it is hard to collect ripe seed. However, if the fading flowers are picked at the approach of freezing weather and kept in water in the house, the seed ripens indoors.

Scabras have two enemies: a disease that browns the leaves and a gentian worm that invades the flowers and seed heads. An all-purpose spray used about every two weeks usually controls both troubles. They are worth this attention!

G. septémfida is typical of the best summer-flowering group. It makes 6- to 12-inch stems that spray out along the ground or, in some forms, stand upright. Like most gentians, it has opposite leaves clasping the stems, and alternating at right angles. This species has bunches of blue trumpets with fringes between the petals, at the upturned ends of the stems.

It has many forms, many closely related species, many hybrids. All are easy, beautiful, and something to be grateful for, rescuing the midsummer garden from the doldrums. They are not fussy as to soil or position but must not be allowed to dry out or burn up. They can stand a lot of sun but where summers are very hot prefer half shade. The flower stems brown after blooming and should be picked off.

G. sìno-ornàta is considered the easiest of the fall-blooming Himalayan group but objects to lime in the soil, and so far has not grown well for me. It makes stoloniferous stems, easily divided. It bears huge blue trumpets at the ends of 6- to 8-inch stems; the leaves are narrow. In Scotland, where it grows luxuriously, it is even used as a florist's cut flower. This whole group can be propagated from preflowering cuttings taken of some of the shoots as they emerge in the spring.

G. veitchìòrum. According to Bailey's *Hortus Second,*

this is the same as *G. ornata* in the trade. Other authorities, however, now consider it a separate species. As I have grown it, it has short firm foliage and large blue trumpets. The seeds one is able to get are usually *veitchiorum* hybrids, but all are lovely. There are a great many other fine hybrids, Drake's strain being among the best.

G. *vérna*, the little blue spring gentian of the Alps, makes small clumps of little evergreen, pointed leaves with salver-shaped, starry, deep blue flowers an inch or two above them.

The variety *angulòsa (alàta)* is a sturdier form with a heavier, angled calyx. They need a rich, porous soil, can stand sun or partial shade, and should have a top-dressing of gritty soil in spring and fall, or any time they look at all leggy. They come readily from their fine seed, if planted in late winter so that they get the freezing they need. Some growers leave the tiny seedlings until the second year before transplanting them. Others have success moving three or four at a time. As they like "root company," this seems a good idea, and it gives bigger clumps of bloom. The first year's flowers on a single plant are beautiful but not showy.

Gerànium Cranesbill   *Geraniaceae*   Geranium Family

The geraniums used so lavishly on our West Coast as ground covers and in the East as potted plants are, as most gardeners know, really pelargoniums, though they belong to the same family. Here we are discussing the true geraniums, which are quite different. Some are upright and tall, others low, and still others are mat-forming. They can be used on walls or banks, or for edging raised borders where they will drip over pleasantly and bloom for a long time in summer.

G. *cinéreum,* from the Pyrenees, has small gray lobed leaves, and rose-white, striped flowers (or in the variety

90

álbum, pure white). Variety *subcauléscens,* usually listed as a species, has rich American Beauty red flowers with black centers. These are all perennials, not as long lived as some, but where happy they will seed around. They are clump-forming, about 4 inches high, and should be used in choice positions.

G. *fárreri,* from China, is even more delicate in appearance. It grows about 3 inches high and has pale pink flowers hovering over the small clumps. These little geraniums die

down to a bud in winter and have to be marked or otherwise protected from the trowel.

G. *grandiflòrum alpìnum,* from Turkestan, is 8 to 10 inches high, and has large blue flowers with a white center. It is summer-blooming and showy. Mine do not travel but it is sometimes spoken of as invasive.

G. *lancastriénse.* See G. *sanguineum prostratum.*

G. *macrorrhìzum ingwérsen* comes from Macedonia. It has deeply lobed leaves and forms bushy plants 6 inches tall. The leaves have a pleasant pungent odor and take on attractive autumn colorings. The flowers are pale pink, small, come on branching stems, and do not live up to the promise of the leaves.

G. *renárdi* has gray, pebbly-surfaced, scalloped leaves in clumps, from which one expects more than the pale washed-out flowers that appear.

G. *robertiànum* is Herb-Robert, an annual or biennial found growing wild in this country and elsewhere. The finely cut leaves take on interesting rose and red shades in the fall, and with its constant shower of little pink flowers it brightens up any shady spot. It seeds around but doesn't get in the way. Its pungent odor is an added pleasure.

G. sanguíneum is really a group of forms and varieties. Typically, it grows 1 to 1½ feet high with magenta flowers. It has the usual lobed foliage and interesting seed heads. A white form is more compact and very good. *G. sanguineum prostràtum* is better known as the lovely form *G. lancastriénse*.

It is found on the Isle of Walney off the coast of Lancashire, England. Its flat, small, deeply divided leaves have rich pink flowers (pale pink marked with red lines, when you look closely) in late spring and a spattering of them the rest of the summer. There is a whole group of Walney Hybrids, all making low mats of leaves and varying widely from seed in the color of their flowers. One finds pink, rose, purplish, and carmine tones. Some are very rich and interesting. They all have fine autumn color. For a mat on the top of a wall or some other well-drained spot it is a permanent plant, showing a few central leaves and twiggy stems all winter.

G. wallichiànum comes from the Himalayas. It has a vine-like habit, a long blooming season, and prefers part shade. Its pinkish-lavender flowers decorate the 3- to 4-foot streamers in summer and fall.

Globulària Globulariaceae Globularia Family

G. cordifòlia, from southern Europe, is an evergreen, slow-spreading plant with dark green leaves that will make a ground cover in any place not too hot and dry. It bears fluffy

steel-blue balls of flowers on 3-inch stems, a modest plant that gradually wins you over.

G. *incanéscens,* is even nicer. Its leaves are more silvery, its flowers lower, and it increases very slowly but is just as hardy.

Gypsóphila Babys-Breath   Caryophyllaceae Pink Family
The big gypsophilas are an attractive part of any flower border, while the smaller ones have great charm whether on a wall, used as edging, tucked in next to steps, or on terrace or ledge.

G. *cerastoìdes* doesn't look like one's idea of a babys-breath, with its wide foliage in rosettes on creeping stems and

chalk-white flowers, large for a gypsophila, marked with dark lines. It spreads into fine mats and is a lovely plant in every way. Himalayas.

G. *fraténsis* is close to *repens* but is a more concise plant with deeper pink flowers.

G. *rèpens,* found in both the Alps and the Pyrenees, makes 6-inch mounds of narrow silvery-gray leaves and is

93

covered most of the summer with its good pink or white flowers in airy sprays.

W *Heliánthemum* Sun-Rose   *Cistaceae* Rockrose Family
The helianthemums are low shrubby plants growing up to 12 inches tall. They do well in sunny, well-drained locations. Walls or raised edgings suit them best. Here they can droop over and fill weeks in summer with their "wild roses" in white, yellow, pink, red, and intermediate shades. Their firm narrow leaves with noticeable midveins are frequently dull gray, but they can be wide and glossy green, or anywhere between the two. There are a great many hybrids. Most of those grown in northern gardens are *H. nummulàrium (H. vulgàre)* and its hybrids. They thrive in good loam and do not like starvation.

Hepática Liverleaf   *Ranunculaceae* Crowfoot Family
Hepaticas are among our best-loved woodland plants. It is advisable to buy or collect them in bloom so as to secure the most desirable forms and colors—some produce only puny stars or wishy-washy colors, but the best are full, round-cupped blooms in lovely colors such as white, blue, purple, and sometimes pink. The central decorative tuft of stamens is more prominent in some than in others.

Hepaticas grow in any shady spot that is not parched but prefer a rich woodland soil. Their early bloom and attractive foliage, which remains good all the growing season and well into the winter, suggest their use near the house where they can be appreciated through their various stages. Interplanted with primroses, which they precede in bloom, and perhaps

94

with hardy cyclamen for later color and interesting foliage, one small area can make a series of beautiful pictures.

There are European forms. Our American species are *H. acutíloba* and *americàna (H. tríloba)*. There is little difference between them except in the shape of leaf.

Heuchèra Coral-Bells   *Saxifragaceae* (Saxifrage Family).

Heucheras have much to recommend them. They are native plants that have been extensively hybridized. Above their clumps of rather round, scalloped leaves they send up flowering sprays from late spring through most of the summer. These can be white, pink, red, and intermediate shades. Most of those grown in gardens are *H. sanguínea* or its hybrids. They do best in good loam and, depending upon the soil, can be anywhere from 10 inches to 2 feet high or more.

Hieràcium Hawkweed   *Compositae* Composite Family

H. bombycìnum. The very name hawkweed fills most gardeners with horror—they are pretty enough with their yellow to orange flowers and low clumps of hairy leaves, but how they spread! However, this species from Spain is a really

good member of a weedy group. It has excessively hairy, gray leaves in neat clumps and good, clear yellow, 6-inch-high flowers, opening successively over a long period in late spring and summer.

Hippocrèpis Hippocrepis   *Leguminosae* Pulse Family
  H. comòsa is a creeper from the Mediterranean region.
It has dark green pinnate leaves that cling to rock or bank and
root freely. In late spring it has crowns of yellow pea flowers

over a long period. It is supposed to prefer sun, but mine do
best in half shade. It makes a fine ground cover and is readily
divided. Some warn against its invasiveness but it has behaved
well here. There is also a double form.

Houstònia Bluets   *Rubiaceae* Madder Family
  H. caerùlea is a beloved native that grows about 6 inches
high and in early spring covers its neat mounds of small leaves
with appealing cool blue or white flowers. It likes a moist
location and there will seed around pleasantly. There are a
number of species, some found in dry woods.

Hutchinsia Hutchinsia   *Cruciferae* Mustard Family

H. alpìna. This little mountain flower grows only an inch or two high but spreads into good mats of dark green, lobed leaves with pure white flowers over a long period in spring

and early summer. It prefers half shade and ample moisture, and, considering its size, is a showy and most attractive addition to our plantings.

Hypéricum St. Johnswort   *Hypericaceae*

St. Johnswort Family

There are a great many hypericums ranging from roadside weeds through shrubby little plants to shrubs 2 to 4 feet high. The flowers are invariably yellow with a noticeable brush of golden stamens. Not all are hardy in cold climates. They bloom in late spring and summer.

H. còris from the Maritime Alps, is a little beauty with excessively fine, narrow foliage spaced closely on the stems. Its golden flowers are streaked with red.

H. olýmpicum is a lovely one from southern Europe. It has smooth, grayish-green narrow leaves on 10-inch stems,

topped by large golden flowers with their big bunches of stamens.

H. polyphýllum, from Cilicia, has smaller leaves growing noticeably in four ranks along the stems. It has a more drooping habit than *olympicum* and somewhat smaller flowers. Fine for hanging over a rock or wall.

Hypóxis   Yellow-Eyed Grass   *Amaryllidaceae*

Amaryllis Family

H. hirsùta. This little native may sometimes be found along roadsides and on the edges of woods. Its bright yellow flowers, although only one or two are open at a time, provide a cheerful note whether in the wild or in your garden. It is

absolutely hardy and will grow in full sun but blooms persistently through the summer if given part shade and adequate moisture. Although it calls to mind the blue-eyed grass *(Sisyrinchium),* a comparison of the sketches will show the wide difference in growth.

Ibèris   Hardy Candytuft   *Cruciferae*   Mustard Family

The hardy candytufts are really small evergreen shrubs native to the Mediterranean region. They will usually come through the hardest winter unscathed. If they are hurt, a good clipping back will start them off again. They are indispensable both for their year-round dark green foliage and their fine flowers, usually brilliant white. Their varying heights and habits fit them for a variety of positions.

I. gibraltárica is the least hardy of the perennial kinds.

Sometimes it acts like a biennial. It has showy pinkish-lavender flowers on foot high plants.

I. jucúnda is another name for *Aethionema coridifolium*.

I. pygmaèa is said to be a horticultural name. It is, however, a distinct plant with very fine foliage; it grows horizontally, and has rather flat heads of white flowers. It is per-

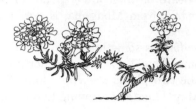

fect for wall decoration or among other fine plants on ledges or banks where it blooms in spring.

I. saxátilis is like a slightly larger *pygmaea,* 3 to 4 inches high, with larger flowers over a long period in spring.

I. semperflòrens is a grand wall plant but needs a couple of feet of space. Its sheets of white in spring are followed by intermittent blooming the rest of the season. Even in winter it may open a flower or two. A good shearing after the spring burst of bloom keeps it from getting leggy and out of bounds.

I. sempervìrens is lower and less rampant. It is a good accent shrub or makes an excellent low hedge 12 to 15 inches

high. It is one of the parents of the many hybrids listed as Little Gem, Snowflake, etc. Little Gem has very narrow, fine foliage, and makes neat bushes 6 to 8 inches high. Snowflake is of medium height with large flowers like *sempervirens*. There are many intermediate forms and hybrids as well as other species, all of which bloom in late spring.

Iris Iris   *Iridaceae* Iris Family

This is an enormous group of plants of inestimable value
for gardens. There are two main divisions of iris, bulbous and
rhizomatous. Those with rhizomes are divided into three
classes, the pogon or bearded group, the apogon or beardless,
and the crested or evansia. The last have a ridge or crest instead of a beard on their lower petals or falls.

I. arenària, from Mongolia, is now usually considered to
be *I. flavíssima.*

I. bloudòwi is sometimes also listed as a variety of *flavissima.* It comes from Turkestan and north China and for garden
purposes the two plants are very close. They are both dwarf,
bloom in May, *bloudowi* growing to 6 inches, *flavissima* to 3 or
4. Both have lovely, rather flat, small, yellow flowers over
narrow leaves. In form they look like a crested iris but a yellow
beard on the falls places them in that group. The flowers are
short-lived but new ones open each morning over a long period in spring. A location on top of a wall or on a well-drained
bank in sun suits them.

*I. chameìris.*This and *I. pùmila,* like the two above, are
easily confused. They have botanical differences. *Chamaeiris,*
the taller of the two, comes from France and Italy, *pumila* from
Austria, Russia, and Asia Minor. Both have been hybridized
freely and when you raise them from seed, as I do, it is hard to
see much difference. Both are small bearded versions of the big
German bearded iris. They may grow 3 to 12 inches high.
Originally their colors were yellow, white, and shades of purple
but now endless tones and colors may be had. *I. pumila
atroviolàcea* flowers in mid-April. It is the earliest of the group
to bloom in this garden. Very small, its 3- to 4-inch high reddish
purple flowers give the effect of stained glass when seen against
the sun. All are easy plants for masses of color anywhere in
spring.

I. chrysógraphes, from China, 15 to 18 inches high, has
very narrow leaves. The form I have has long black buds contrasting beautifully with the pale green leaves; these develop
into deep purple, beardless flowers with velvety falls, veined
yellow. It likes moisture and half shade and does well at the
foot of a wall where it blooms in June.

I. cristàta is a most appealing little iris, a native that blooms in mid-May. Its broad low leaves, about 6 inches high,

fan out from rhizomes that hump along the ground in a characteristic way. The little flowers are soft blue with white and yellow crest. The white form is a bit larger in all its parts and like so many white flowers usually blooms ahead of the type. They like good soil in half shade but will grow and bloom more prolifically in sun, if their roots are under or between rocks where the ground stays cool and damp.

I. douglasiàna is one of a large group of so-called California iris, though their range goes through Oregon and Washington. I have grown many of them at different times and all were much to be desired. So far *douglasiana* has been the most permanent. It comes in many colors. Mine is a delicious raspberry with large flowers on 15- to 18-inch stems. This whole group is beardless and blooms in spring.

The Dutch iris are bulbous and all are hybrids. Their very narrow, almost grasslike foliage is topped by flowers on 15-inch stems. They may be white, yellow, or wonderful tones of blue. They make an excellent cut flower, and bloom in late spring.

I. flavíssima. See *I. bloudowi.*

I. fórresti is another Chinese beardless iris, a good companion for *chrysographes*, since they like the same cool location. It is one of my favorites, growing 12 to 15 inches high with soft yellow flowers in June.

I. gracílipes is a delicate little crested beauty from Japan. The fans of narrow leaves rise about 8 inches and the pinkish-

lilac flowers float above them on their fine stems in May. It thrives in light woodland soils in half shade and is much stronger than it looks. There is also a white form.

I. gramínea **and** *síntenisi* are two more iris that are very close from a gardener's point of view. Both are Europeans, beardless, with tight clumps of narrow leaves from 6 to 12 inches high and usually less than half an inch wide. Just topping the leaves, or sometimes among them, are the delicate purple flowers, the falls veined with white and purple, the standards reddish purple in *graminea*, bluish purple in *sintenisi*. In general, the shape of the flowers reminds one of *reticulata*. In addition, *graminea* is supposed to smell of ripe plums. This characteristic does not seem to be constant. Like sweet violets they need the sun or a certain time of day to send forth their fragrance. They bloom in June and though they never shout at you both have exquisite beauty.

I. pùmila. See *I. chamaeiris.*

I. reticulàta is a bulbous one from the Caucasus. It has square reedlike leaves up to 8 inches tall and purple flowers smelling like sweet violets. They are among the earliest

flowers to bloom in spring; they defy March storms. There are several forms and a companion bulb with yellow flowers called *I. dánfordiae*.

I. síntenisi. See *I. graminea.*

I. tectòrum, from China, is better known as the roof iris of Japan. It has fans of broad leaves about 8 inches high and carried well above them are the large, flat, crested flowers of fine lavender or orchidlike white. The latter is often spoken of as the "rare white form," but I have found it just as easy as the type. It blooms in mid-May, followed by the lavender species. They are among the loveliest of iris. It is advisable to lift and divide them every two years after blooming.

I. vérna is a beardless native of the eastern states, a precious 3-inch beauty with pale to deep blue flowers with a dash of gold. In peaty, humusy soil in part shade it is one of the thrills of spring. It is not an easy iris unless given the proper

103

soil and location. *I. cristata* is often considered a good substitute.

Jasiòne Jasione   *Campanulaceae* Bluebell Family
    J. perénnis. This European plant makes clumps of hairy narrow leaves that give rise to tall, branching flower stems 12 to 15 inches high. The steel-blue heads of flowers look at

first like cornflowers, then gradually develop into a fluffy ball that is really a collection of flowers. In drawing these plants I look at them first through a magnifying glass to find out what makes them look that way. It is amazing. We miss half the interest and beauty of our flowers looking at them without such an aid. At any rate, jasione is a valuable addition to our gardens. It blooms in late June and July (so is doubly welcome) and, if the fading flowers are cut off, the side branches keep blooming for ever so long.

104

Lavándula Lavender   *Labiatae* Mint Family

L. officinális is the sweet lavender of the Mediterranean region. Remembering this, we give it a warm sunny position in our gardens, preferably snuggled between rocks. There it will live as a 3-foot shrub year after year, filling the hot

summer days with fragrance and with the beauty of its rich violet or lavender flowers. There is also a pale pink form and a white. Variety *compácta* is the *nàna* of catalogs. With me it has lived on top of a wall for years, coming through difficult winters unscathed. It grows 1 foot high and 2 feet wide. If you can bear to cut your lavender flowers in full bloom, you can dry them on newspapers in the attic or other warm space, then strip the flowers for sachets.

Leontopòdium Edelweiss   *Compositae*

Composite Family

L. alpìnum. Some, I imagine, really like the white, woolly edelweiss of the Alps, while others will only say, "*That* is the edelweiss!" My own opinion is that the 6-inch plant has little to recommend it, since it is flannelly and featureless and lacks fragrance and color. In any case, it will live a few years in very well drained gritty soil in sun.

Lewisia Lewisia   *Portulacaceae* Purslane Family
Lewisia has a different story to tell. These are among the most beautiful flowers we can grow. The evergreen ones are worth a place for their leaves alone. They are all natives and something to take pride in.

They need a lime-free, sandy, peaty, well-drained soil in part shade. They do best planted vertically in a crevice of rock or wall where no water can stand on the crown. They are not difficult to raise from seed, given the needed freezing by late winter planting. They are, however, slow to develop into blooming plants, are fussy when young, needing perfect drainage, shade, and top-dressing with stone chips or gravel at every stage.

L. cotylèdon. These are evergreen plants with glossy rosettes. I have grown only the hybrids. The one pictured has

apricot flowers striped with pink and is enchanting. It grows 6 to 8 inches high. There are a number of evergreen species, some with crimped or waved leaf edges: *fínchi, héckneri, hòwelli,* and *tweèdyi.* The last named has much larger salmon-pink flowers.

L. redivìva is deciduous. It is called bitter-root and is the state flower of Montana. It has odd, reddish, thick roots 1 to

3 inches long. In spring they send up cylindrical leaves to an inch or two. These die down and then up come large cactus-like flowers of a fine pink. When these fade the leaves reappear and remain until late fall. The roots are likely to be heaved out by frost and so lost; otherwise it is hardy. It will grow in sun or part shade.

Linària Toadflax *Scrophulariaceae* Figwort Family

L. alpìna is a most lovable little plant that really should be shown in color. Its blue-gray foliage contrasts so pleasantly with its purple, orange-marked flowers with their rabbit ears sticking straight up. It makes a 6-inch mound of delicate stems

and leaves, and one finds a few flowers in bloom almost any time. There is a pretty pink form and many hybrids. The latter are taller and straighter, up to 8 inches tall, and have slightly larger flowers, nearer to the wild butter-and-eggs, which was undoubtedly one of the parents. They come in many odd and interesting colors but none are as attractive as *alpina*. They are much more persistent, however. *Alpina* is not reliably hardy but will seed around where happy, so that you rarely lose it entirely.

Lìnum Flax *Linaceae* Flax Family

L. alpìnum is a low plant, about 6 inches high and a foot wide. It has the same fine foliage but the blue flowers are more persistent than *perenne* and the other tall blue flaxes. It is a lovely species that blooms for a long time in spring.

L. flàvum is a European. There are several yellow flaxes, but from seed they all seem to turn out much alike, some merely growing taller than others. They are all a bit woody at the base and grow up to 8 to 12 inches high, with fine bluish-

green leaves and luscious clear yellow flowers in late spring. The one pictured is *flavum compáctum.*

   L. perénne, narbonnénse, lèwisi, and others are all very close, the first two being Europeans, the last an American. In some the petals overlap or may have a touch of red, or be a deeper blue, but there are hybrids among them too. They are

all airy plants, growing 18 inches to 2 feet high, covered each morning with a cloud of blue flowers. By afternoon these drop but the next morning there is the cloud again, giving a lift to the June garden. When they begin to go too much to seed it is advisable to cut the whole plant back to about 6 inches. It will then make a mound of soft new leaves and persist over the winter. Otherwise, the plant is likely to bloom itself to death.

Lòtus Birds-Foot Trefoil   *Leguminosae* Pulse Family
   L. corniculàtus. The seeds of this plant have been imported from Europe for extensive planting along the banks of some of our highways, notably, the Pennsylvania Turnpike.

This gives us a hint on how to use it in our gardens. It can stand heat and drought and thrives on shearing. The leaves are a fine dark green while the pealike flowers are butter yellow. They bloom most of the summer. In level rich soil it is inclined to grow too lush but on a bank in the sun its drooping habit is encouraged. It is easily propagated from seed, division, or cuttings.

Lýchnis Campion   *Caryophyllaceae* Pink Family
   These are mostly Europeans and not outstanding but they have their uses. *L. alpìna*, a little one, adds a bright if somewhat magenta note to the spring garden. *L. Coronària* has escaped to this country, and its crimson flowers on 2- to 3-foot stems, over white woolly leaves, are likely to come up in any garden. *L. Flós-jòvis* has fine pink flowers on 8-inch stems over woolly gray leaves but is not a very long-lived perennial. The

109

only other one I grow is *L. sártori,* a foot high over 3-inch clumps of green leaves. The flowers vary from white to deep pink. It is a persistent perennial.

Màzus Mazus   *Scrophulariaceae*   Figwort Family
     M. réptans comes from Asia but has made itself very much at home in this country. It is a valuable ground cover for moist cool soil in sun or half shade. It cannot be allowed among select company, for its thick mats root as they run. In the joints of paving stones on a shady terrace it is superb; in wet ground it will make a heavenly lawn covered with its lavender bloom.

It can compete successfully with grass, clover, and other spreaders such as *Veronica filiformis.* This, be it understood, is a lawn for the gods, not for the suburbanite whose ideal is a golfing green!

Merténsia Bluebells   *Boraginaceae*   Borage Family
     In addition to the big Virginia bluebells with their pink

110

and blue flowers that grow in wet meadows, in woodlands, or in gardens, there are a number of charming dwarf, native species from our West. *M. longiflòra* is a choice one of these, growing 3 to 8 inches high. It has glaucous blue leaves and in early spring hangs out its pale blue, pink-budded, flowers.

Woodland soil and half shade suit it. It disappears over winter. In its dormant state it is a dried-out looking little corm that doesn't look as though it could possibly sprout—and sometimes it doesn't.

Mitchélla Partridge-Berry *Rubiaceae* Madder Family
   M. rèpens is a wonderful evergreen ground cover for part shade. Native to North America, it spreads about sparsely in the woods, but on a bank at the edge of the woods or in another well-drained half-shady place it will soon make thick

mats of its small, glossy, dark green leaves. In spring the fuzzy white flowers, deep pink in bud, exhale a delicate fragrance. These are followed by bright red berries that the birds may find before you do.

Myosòtis Forget-Me-Not   *Boraginaceae*   Borage Family

   M. alpéstris is now the name for the plant formerly called *rupícola*. It is a much smaller, denser plant than *M. sylvatica*. Its short-leaved mats are only a few inches wide and an inch or so high, while the flowers are a deeper blue. It is a lovely little plant but not quite so easy to keep around permanently. Seed is only rarely offered for sale.

   M. scorpioìdes, from Europe and Asia, is an old friend (*M. palústris*). In the variety *semperflòrens* it keeps on blooming all summer. It likes to be on a moist bank but will grow right in a stream and make great mats and hummocks and ribbons of its flopping stems covered with blue, pink-budded flowers. It is less rampant in somewhat drier positions.

   M. sylvática (*M. alpìna* or *alpéstris*). By whatever name, this is our lovely spring forget-me-not, a native of Europe and Asia, but widely grown in our gardens. It can be 3 inches tall or 12, and blue, pink, or white. It also has many named varieties. It is not reliably perennial but you will always have it with you if you allow it to seed around. At Cloud Hill the plants are pulled up when they have gone to seed and shaken around. They promptly make seedlings that live over the winter and fill the spring with their special brand of joy.

Oenothèra Evening Primrose   *Onagraceae*
                              Evening Primrose Family
   O. frèmonti, American like all the rest of them, has nar-

row, silky, silvery leaves and the usual four-petaled yellow-silk flowers. It grows about a foot high but has a drooping habit and when mature needs a couple of feet of space. It starts blooming in June with flowers that may be 2 inches across and is nonstop the rest of the season, nor does it wait for evening to open its flowers. Its manner of growth suggests a raised position, in sun, of course, where it is a permanent plant.

There are many other species, both larger and smaller, and many are biennial. *Missouriénsis*, also hardy, is somewhat like *fremonti*, with green leaves and even larger flowers.

Omphalòdes   Blue-Eyed-Mary   *Boraginaceae*
Borage Family

O. cappadócica is more concise than *verna* and does not creep but it has the same fine flowers and likes similar locations.

O. vérna, from Austria, makes a pleasant, permanent ground cover in shade, as it creeps slowly around. Its large,

rather rough leaves, up to 6 inches long, and its airy sprays of dark blue forget-me-nots are good companions for primroses.

Papàver Poppy   *Papaveraceae* Poppy Family

P. alpìnum. The little alpine poppy, from 3 to 6 inches high, is a delicate beauty in both leaf and flower. Blooming in spring, it has not been a long-lived perennial here but it is worth every effort to establish. It should seed around where it is

113

happy—in gritty, well-drained soil in sun. The colors vary; the one illustrated was a soft apricot.

P. rupífragum. This is a permanent perennial from Spain. Its leaves form clumps of 6-inch gray, hairy, deeply cut leaves. Well above them, on stems to 15 inches long, are orange flowers, an inch or so across. They bloom all through June and into July. As the early spring bloom in the garden fades the morning picture is made gay by the orange poppies and blue flax. By afternoon they have both dropped their petals but the flowers are there again the following morning. This is one poppy that, once established, can be moved with impunity, if the whole root is taken up with all the soil it will hold. It is indifferent to soil or location and seeds around but not excessively.

Penstèmon Beard-Tongue *Scrophulariaceae*

Figwort Family

An American group, the penstemons are legion. There are some native to the East but most of the choice ones are westerners. Some are difficult to establish in eastern gardens. Gabrielson, in *Western American Alpines,* discussed them at length. The American Penstemon Society has been studying them for years, disseminating seed, distributing literature, and publicizing their many virtues. I have grown quantities from seed. Some proved biennial, some just didn't like it here, and some were too large for my garden. As I look around, aside

114

from some nice little shrubby ones not yet in bloom, I can report only on the following:

P. digitàlis is an easterner and will take possession of any place you plant it. It grows 3 feet high and bears spires of good white flowers, some washed with lavender or pink. These are excellent cut flowers. A good plant for a wild garden.

P. fruticòsus. I have low, rather prostrate forms of this woody shrub that have lived on a wall and a slope for years. Some of the wood is winterkilled but new growth and large lavender flowers appear each spring.

P. hirsùtus is a 12-inch easterner with purplish or washed out lavender flowers. Mrs. Henry has worked with this group and has established some good pinks and purples. However, I find they take the garden, if given a chance.

P. jóhnsonae (Flathead Lake) is a fairly recent introduction from the West with good coral-red flowers on 12-inch plants in the dwarf form and 2-foot plants (with sometimes

purple tones) in the larger form. The low ones, with their fine coral flowers and glossy leaves, are an excellent June addition to the garden. I find that annual division prolongs their life.

P. pinifòlius. I show a seedling of this and one other little shrubby one to emphasize the differences in form among

115

penstemons. *Pinifolius* grows 9 inches high with good red flowers in summer.

Phlóx Phlox   *Polemoniaceae* Polemonium Family

This is an American family. How could we do without it? Leaving aside the tall, perennial, border phlox, some of the best are:

P. divaricàta. The woods or Canadian phlox is one of the indispensables. It grows about a foot high with slowly creeping rootstocks, low stems of narrow leaves that in some forms are not conspicuous, and which "helpers" might weed out when not in bloom. It shows its lovely lavender, 1-inch flowers in big clusters for a long season, through both daffodil and tulip time. It is a perfect foil for any other color. It will grow in sun or shade making a ground cover in the woods or seeding over a sunny garden. It is easily pulled out if it encroaches on other plants but I seldom have too much of it.

P. nivàlis. This looks much like the *subulata* phloxes but has fewer leaves, grows a little taller and more openly, and has larger flowers, up to 1 inch. In addition, it blooms a bit later, thus extending the season. A fine form with rich pink flowers is called Camla, and there are other named varieties, some white, some near red.

P. procúmbens has small glossy leaves, not needlelike, and bright pink flowers on 6-inch plants. It blooms with or ahead of the *subulatas* in spring. It is a fine plant, though some might find the pink color a bit strong.

P. stolonífera (P. réptans) has larger, glossier, more rounded leaves and even lovelier lavender flowers (in the best form) than *divaricata*. Its prostrate stems spread by stolons.

116

It needs a rich, peaty soil in part shade, where it will make a fine ground cover. There is a deep pink form, not as good.

P. subulàta. Mountain pink is the local name for this fine stand-by. Its sheets of needlelike leaves are evergreen, valuable as a ground cover winter and summer. There are many forms and hybrids with much variety of color to choose from. Many spread too fast for small gardens or placement near choice plants. A slow-growing, compact variety is *brittoni,* a

charmer with white or soft pink flowers. The variety Vivid makes 4-inch mounds and is one of the most valuable. Its flowers are a rich pink without a trace of magenta, and they have a darker eye. It makes clumps rather than mats and doesn't get out of hand.

Physària Physaria   *Cruciferae* Mustard Family

P. didymocárpa. This little plant from our Northwest has a 1-inch clump of silver leaves and just the right tone of pale yellow flowers to set them off. In gritty soil in a wall it is proving hardy at Cloud Hill. A delightful spring-blooming morsel.

117

Phyteùma   Hornèd Rampion   *Campanulaceae*

Bluebell Family

P. sièberi, from Europe, shows its relationship to the
campanulas more in the leaves, which have the same firm
texture and shape as many of its relatives, than in its odd blue
flowers. They look even more unusual under a magnifying

glass, though there you can see that the flowers making up
the head are five-parted. It is permanent, gradually increasing
the clumps and the number of flowers, so that its soft purplish-

118

blue tone is effective. It is not fussy with regard to location, though it does best in part shade. It blooms in June.

Polemònium Jacobs-Ladder *Polemoniaceae*

Phlox Family

There are ladders from 1 inch to 3 feet, almost all of them native to our West and most of them soft blue. All are pleasant to have around, a few are little beauties.

P. pulchérrimum starts like the 2-inch plant pictured but the leaves eventually grow about 6 inches long. Its beautiful

leaves are further enhanced by the flowers. It blooms in late spring and is perfectly hardy in part shade.

P. réptans grows a foot or so high and with its creeping habit makes a good ground cover in any half-shady place. Its sprays of flowers are blue or white. It also blooms in late spring.

Potentilla Cinquefoil *Rosaceae* Rose Family

This a very large group. Many are weeds and many are among the most useful and attractive garden flowers. Some have leaves and flowers recalling the strawberry, though the colors vary widely.

P. álba, from Europe, has palmate leaves up to 4 inches and delicate, flat, white flowers. Even the stamens are white, springing from an orange-colored ring at the base. It never

119

blooms profusely but starts in early spring and has a few flowers almost all the time.

P. ambígua comes from the Himalayas and has very glossy, strongly veined, small, three-parted leaves, deeply toothed at the ends. It is a slowly creeping plant with half-inch yellow flowers. It should have a front position where its good qualities can be appreciated.

P. atrosanguínea, also Himalayan, has typical strawberry leaves with a silver lining that shows at the edges. The flowers, bright red, bloom in May on stems that spray around for 12 to 15 inches. I have seedlings of a new *atrosanguinea* (still with a number instead of a name) that is said to have flowers from dark maroon through crimson and pink to pale sulphur yellow.

P. eriocárpa, still another Himalayan, is entirely different. It bloomed the first year from seed on tiny pale silvery-green plants, the leaves three-parted and notched at the ends. It

creeps gently about and raises pale yellow flowers a bit above the foliage. It is not long-lived but may seed itself in congenial surroundings—meaning sun, gritty soil, and perfect drainage.

P. fragifórmis comes from Siberia. The big soft velvety three-parted leaves make a mat above which very large yellow flowers are borne. The leaves would be sufficiently attractive in themselves. It develops slowly from seed and prefers a cool damp position in sun or part shade, where it brightens the garden in May.

P. fruticòsa, a widely distributed shrub, grows to 3 feet and has yellow flowers flecked over it for much of the summer. More attractive are its smaller varieties (most of them from China), and their many hybrids. These shrubs are 1 to 2 feet high, with small leaves and flowers from white through pale to deep golden yellow. They are all long-blooming summer plants and make fine accents for garden, border, terrace, or colorful low hedge.

P. nepalénsis, from the Himalayas, has five-fingered leaves and flowers in sprays on long stems in various shades of raspberry. It blooms in July. The variety Miss Wilmott is lower, growing up to only 12 inches, but plants from seed do not always keep this characteristic.

P. nevadénsis, from Spain, is a prostrate creeping plant with soft gray five-parted leaves and early-blooming pale, glowing yellow flowers that almost hide the leaves when in bloom. In damp weather some of the foliage may rot but there are always divisions to carry on.

P. nítida, from the Alps, I have had for years. Its small, silvery, silky three-parted leaves, toothed at the ends, wander around without the slightest intention of blooming for me. The flowers should be single pink "roses"—the beauty of the race. We are warned to starve this high alpine to make it bloom. I feed it only stone chips still no flowers.

P. rupéstris is another European. It sprays around to 8 inches with leaves like a geum and flowers like a strawberry in early spring. Variety *pygmaèa* is a daintier version.

P. tormentíllo-formòsa (P. tónguei) is a hybrid with five-fingered leaves and a drooping habit. The small leaves make a central rosette from which streamers a foot long produce its red-centered apricot flowers. It should be placed to take advantage of this habit of growth; it will bloom most of the summer.

P. tridentàta is a native with three-parted leaves, glossy and decorative, but not much enhanced by its sprays of very small white flowers, though they bloom most of the summer too.

P. vérna nàna, from Europe, makes flat mats of its five-parted leaves, then is covered by its small, bright, golden flowers in spring. It is a creeper and can be readily divided.

Primula Primrose   *Primulaceae*   Primrose Family

The huge, wonderful primrose family is the stand-by of the shady garden, whether grown in woodlands, as carpeting under shrubs, planted along the waterside, used near the house, or anywhere in the garden where there is some shade for the hottest part of the day. There are so many primulas in the world that, for convenience, they have been divided into sections according to type. The study of all the primulas in all the sections is for the specialist or for those who can provide the special conditions that some of them require. Here are mentioned only those groups most commonly grown. It is a help to know to which section a given plant belongs, for the growing requirements are usually common to the group.

The *Aurícula* Section includes *P. auricula* and other European alpine primroses and their hybrids. Their need is for stony, well-drained, rich, loamy soil, lightened by leaf mold and sand. They can stand more sun than most of the primulas but in our climate prefer protection from hot midday sun. They like to get their roots under stones and to be top-dressed with stone chips. They are usually evergreen and bloom in early spring.

The *Candelábra* Section, from Asia, is easy to identify. The flowers grow in tiers, one whorl above another, and are open-faced and looking at you. Most are tall plants with big leaves. All want moist soil in part shade. They bloom in late spring and early summer and disappear over winter.

The *Capitàtae* Section is from the Himalayas. These are biennial here but not necessarily so in other climates. In colder climates where the snow stays as a cover all winter many primulas survive that can't stand the constant freezing and thawing that we get. They are also perennial on the West Coast. This is true of all those I speak of as biennial here. They are all so lovely, they should be tried out in varying conditions. The *capitatas* bloom late, about July, and have rather flat rosettes of delicately toothed leaves and foot-high silver stems bearing rather flat, silvery heads of slightly drooping flowers. They disappear over winter.

122

The *Cortusoìdes* Section come from Asia. They are woodland plants, thus indicating a rich humusy soil. They have decorative leaves varying in form but usually softly hairy. They, too, disappear over winter. They bloom in spring.

The *Denticulàta* Section. These, too, come from the Himalayas, a small group that is easy, perennial, and only have to be guarded against excessive winter damp. They leave a large bud at the surface over winter and are among the earliest flowers of spring.

The *Farinòsae* Section is a huge group from many lands. They need moisture, good drainage, and partial shade, though they will grow in sun if kept moist enough. They leave a small bud, usually white, at the surface over winter.

The *Nivàlis* Section, from Asia, is biennial here. They have long narrow leaves, mealy underneath. Their flowers grow in closer tiers than the *candelabras* and have a more drooping habit. They need a cool rich moist soil in part shade; they bloom in early spring and disappear over winter.

The *Sikkiménsis* Section is also from Asia. They are called belled primulas, because they all have hanging heads of bell-shaped flowers. They are biennial here but are reported perennial in colder or warmer climates. Most of them are tall with heads of fragrant flowers held well above the large, toothed leaves. They bloom in late spring and disappear over winter.

4/79 • The *Vernàles* Section includes all the best-known and most easily grown primroses. They prefer part shade and rich soil, sufficiently moist so that they never dry out entirely. They fill the spring with glory: *P. vulgàris (P. acaùlis)*, the polyanthas with their many forms, and the *jùliae* Hybrids. They are evergreen.

P. acaùlis. See *P. vulgaris.*

P. alpícola, of the *sikkimensis* section grows up to 20 inches but there is also a dwarf form. It is very fragrant with one-sided sprays of pale yellow flowers, with white and purple varieties.

P. atrodentàta is a dwarf *denticulata* but not as surely permanent.

P. aurantiàca is a rather small member of the *candelabras.* It grows 12 to 14 inches high and has red flower buds that

123

4.79.
Primula
abbreviata
See Vernalis.
12 plants
fr. Winterthur.
— also
v. Cowichans
Victorians
Julia v.
wanda
Veris

open into yellow or orange flowers. The midrib of the leaves is also red, the whole a most lovely addition to the garden. It has an odd habit of forming a cluster of small leaves at the top of the flower stalk. This will bend over and root, or it can be detached and grown as a cutting.

P. auricula. The wild *auricula* of the Alps is one thing, the *auriculas* you see in gardens are something else. The original *auricula* is a fragrant, yellow, mealy-leaved plant found growing in rock crevices. It is 2 to 4 inches high. It is very hard to get the original form.

Modern *auriculas* are all hybrids. Their growing became a cult long ago in England and it is rapidly becoming one in this country. They have been divided into three classes: Show, Alpine, and Garden *auriculas.* The Show *auricula* is just that, not for outdoor culture. The Alpine *auricula,* like the Show

auricula, has definite standards of perfection towards which the devotees strive; for example, flat flowers, rounded petals, yellow or cream center, and even shading of the flower from dark to light. Garden *auriculas* are just well-formed flowers on sturdy stems and can be almost any color. The clumps multiply by offsets and can be readily divided.

P. bulleyàna is a tall *candelabra*. The coloring is much like *P. aurantiaca,* and it is a remarkably handsome plant.

P. burmánica is a fine purple *candelabra* with a yellow eye. It makes a good foil for the lighter colored species.

P. cachemiriàna is a variety of *denticulata,* somewhat smaller and with fine lavender flowers.

P. capitàta mooreàna is sometimes listed as *P. mooreàna.* The purple, slightly drooping, very fragrant flowers, with silvered calyxes and stems, are exceptionally lovely. The rather flat head first opens a ring of flowers, then central buds develop into additional ones. They are held well above the mat of thin toothed leaves with rounded ends. It is deciduous and biennial here.

P. carniólica is a little 4-inch plant in the *auricula* section, with glossy leaves and umbels of pink to lilac, white-centered flowers. It wants a cool location where it can spread into big mats.

P. chionántha. This is a white *nivalis,* fragrant and lovely, but not long-lived here.

P. chrysòpa (P. gemmífera zambalénsis) is another of the *farinosae* group with small leaves and pink flowers on 6- to 8-inch stems. Perennial but not very long-lived, it does best in cool shade.

P. clusiàna is a white-eyed, pink to lilac species in the *auricula* section. It has notched petals and glossy green leaves, grows 3 to 4 inches high. It is considered one of the easiest of this group.

P. darialìca is very close to *P. farinosa.*

P. denticulàta can be white, pink, rose, red, lavender, or purple. It starts blooming at the first breath of spring, with round heads on short stems, among short leaves. As the season advances the stems and leaves lengthen. The flowers may grow a foot high and after they fade the leaves make a big head like romaine salad. It is readily divided after blooming or in early fall, or can be left to increase its girth each year. It should be

in every garden, in woods, against a rock, or anywhere that it won't get waterlogged in winter.

P. elàtior is the European oxlip, of the *vernales* section. It grows 6 to 8 inches high with small yellow flowers in umbels,

a charming plant. It has hybrids with larger flowers and varying colors.

P. farinòsa, the birdseye primrose, is the type plant of its section. It is a small plant, 3 to 6 inches high, or in the *scótica* form, 2 inches. The leaves, about 2 inches long, are coated with white meal underneath, the flowers are delicate pink to purple, in loose umbels, with a yellow eye. They bloom in early spring. I find that annual division of the clumps tends to

lengthen their lives and that a ground cover such as *Veronica filiformis* gives them the root company they like. Where wild they are found in moist meadows among grasses.

P. faùriei álba (fauriae) is close to *farinosa*. The white form listed here is a real addition to the garden as white *farinosa* is hard to get. The leaves of *fauriei* are flatter and smoother than *farinosa* and diminish to a footstalk, while the meal on the reverse of the leaves is yellow instead of white.

P. florindae is a large member of the *sikkimensis* section. It can grow 3 to 4 feet high in very wet ground. At Cloud Hill

it grew 18 inches, fragrant with drooping yellow bells, and proved biennial. It has heart-shaped, stalked leaves.

P. frondòsa, from the Balkans, is a larger, sturdier *farinosa.* It increases rapidly, is easy, divisible, and permanent.

P. heucherifòlia is a specially attractive member of the *cortusoides* section. It has rather rounded, lobed, deeply veined leaves with 4-inch stems of hanging crimson flowers. It is spring-blooming and wants the usual woodland conditions of its group.

P. involucràta is another member of the large *farinosae* section. It has no meal on its glossy little leaves. Its fragrant, slightly drooping white flowers are carried on 6-inch stems. It is a plant for a cool moist place and won't stand drying.

127

P. japónica is the type of the *candelabras* to which all others are compared. It is also the easiest and most reliable. It comes in reds, pinks, and white; of the latter Postford White is the best. It will seed around abundantly where its liking for moisture, shade, and cool soil is met. It can be anywhere from 1 to 3 feet high.

P. jùliae. The original *juliae* is a small plant with very small leaves, of creeping habit, and flowers near magenta yet with a jewellike quality that makes it attractive. The original form is hard to find but there are hybrids by the score. These

for some unknown reason are called *julianas*. They can be flat creepers with small leaves like *juliae* or carry stalked flowers, most of which are dainty, or may compete with the *vulgaris* hybrids in size.

They are very hardy, needing only good soil, adequate moisture, occasional top-dressing, and division when necessary. They bloom prolifically in spring with the other *vernales* and have a way of showing a few flowers from time to time. They can be used in foreground plantings with other primroses, or anywhere in light shade that a pool of color is wanted. They come in white and a variety of colors including pink, blue, and yellow.

P. kisoàna is a beautiful member of the *cortusoides* group. Its extremely woolly stems and soft hairy leaves give rise to 6-inch-high pink flowers of good color, lacking the bluish cast

128

of so many of this group. It spreads around pleasantly, is
soundly perennial, and easily divided.

P. luteola belongs to the *farinosae* section, though it has
no farina on the leaves. I had this for several years without a
bloom. It is much too valuable a plant to let go without
another try. The light green, toothed leaves, 3 to 4 inches
long, have a lush, lettucey quality. Well above them they
carry dense heads of pale yellow flowers in July and August.
Rich cool soil and good drainage are recommended.

P. polyántha is the *polyanthus* of gardens, the most popular of the *vernales* section. It differs from *vulgaris (acaulis)* in
having a stalked umbel of flowers well above the foliage,
instead of single flowers on stems, though in some hybrids
you sometimes get the two forms on the same plant. It is supposed to be descended from crosses of *vulgaris*, the cowslip
(veris), and oxlip *(elatior)*, the two latter also having their
flowers in umbels on stalks. It comes in every imaginable color,
with larger and larger flowers, stronger stems, and bigger
leaves. One hopes the hybridizers will stop striving for bigness.

It is very easy to grow when given protection from the
hottest sun and is at its best in woodlands, planted among
other shade-loving flowers, ferns, and bulbs. Division every
two or three years is advisable, or more frequently if you are
in a hurry to increase your plantings. The soil must not be
allowed to wear out, as they are hearty feeders. Many are fragrant, inheriting this grand quality from the cowslip. With the
vernal group you can have a riot of color in spring.

129

Belonging to the *polyanthas* group, we also have the plants known as Gold- and Silver-laced *polyanthas*, Hose-in-

hose, and Jack-in-the-green. The laced polyanthas are also a development of the English florists (most of them weavers interested in floriculture, and not florists as we know them in this country). The ideal they worked toward was a very dark-centered flower with a perfect edging of gold or silver on the round petals. Hybridizers in this country are carrying on. Hose-in-hose plants have one flower growing out of another. In the old ones the flowers were small, usually red and yellow, and had a certain charm. The new developments along this line come in many colors with large flowers, interesting, but not as much fun as the old ones. Jack-in-the-green plants are those that show a ruff of small leaves surrounding the individual flowers in the head. In addition, there are endless hybrids among the *polyanthas*, some dwarf, many showing solid color or velvety tones.

P. polyneùra includes *veìtchi* and others of the *cortusoides* section. They have scalloped leaves, up to 2 inches long and softly hairy, and 8- to 10-inch stems carrying small heads of purplish, crimson, or magenta flowers.

130

P. pubéscens should be written X *pubescens,* the X indicating that they are hybrids. They are crosses between
auricula, rùbra, and others. They are all smaller than the
auriculas and with a less formal appearance. They come in
many colors and named varieties and are at their best in walls,
on ledges, or tucked in close at hand where they won't be
overshadowed by big plants.

P. pulverulénta is a *candelabra* close to *P. japonica* but
with silvered stems and not quite such a strong constitution.

One of the loveliest of all *candelabras* is a warm pink called
Bartley Strain. Like all the *candelabras* these want more shade
than sun and plenty of moisture.

P. ròsea, native to the Himalayas, along streams and
ravines, is of the *farinosae* clan though it doesn't look it. Glossy
small, toothed leaves without farina give rise to 6- to 8-inch
stems of the most luscious rich pink flowers in small loose
heads. There are larger and smaller forms and deeper colored
flowers but all are among the most striking of primulas. It is

131

a very early one, and needs more moisture than the average, though good drainage is still important.

P. saxátilis, of the *cortusoides* section, has sprays of small pinkish flowers in abundance over a long period in spring. It is a very pleasant member of the group, each plant bearing a number of stalks of airy flowers.

P. secundiflòra, from China, is one of the *sikkimensis* section. Its biennial behavior was especially disappointing since it had such lovely drooping wine-colored flowers.

P. sièboldi, from Japan, is the chief member of the *cortusoides* section. It is absolutely perennial, increases its mats of large, decorative, scalloped leaves rapidly, and holds its fine flowers well above the foliage. The flowers may be

pink, white, lavender or two-toned, the reverse of some being a contrasting color. The form of the flowers varies from the usual petal to delicately cut snowflake patterns. It disappears in midsummer after seeding, so must be placed with care. It can be divided just after blooming or when it comes up in spring, though this latter time may prevent flowering that year.

P. vèris (officinàlis) is the cowslip. It is not usually considered good enough for gardens these days. I find it most attractive with its hanging heads of soft yellow flowers and sweet scent. A well-grown plant has showers of flowers. Of

course, there are hybrids of this, too, and the colors may be orange, red, or mixed. It is very easy, permanent, and should have the usual *vernales* treatment.

P. viscòsa, of the *auricula* section, is 4 to 6 inches high with purplish fragrant flowers and leaves with an unpleasant odor. It requires more shade and moisture than most in this section.

P. vulgàris (P. acaùlis), almost last, but far from the least. This is *the* primrose, beloved in the wild in England and on the Continent, hybridized from the pale yellow of the original into rainbow colors. The single flowers are close to the leaves which make increasing mounds. Variety *rùbra* or subspecies *sibthórpi* (sometimes called *altàica*) is the wild Turkish primrose which is a white-eyed, pink flower. The yellow and pink

133

forms started the flood of hybrids. Everything that has been said about the polyantha applies to *vulgaris* too.

    P. yargongénsis is a member of the *farinosae* section, close to *P. involucràta* but with pink to purplish flowers instead of white, and requires the same treatment.

Pterocéphalus Pterocephalus   *Dipsaceae*

                                    Teasel Family

    P. parnássi *(Scabiòsa pterocéphala)* comes from the mountains of Greece. This charming creeper, which gradually enlarges its mats, has soft small gray scalloped leaves and large heads of scabiosa-like flowers, in a cool pale pink. It

blooms for a long time in midsummer especially if the fading flowers are picked off. It is a sturdy perennial, best raised from seed. It will make itself at home on a dry wall or other well-drained spot close at hand where its modest beauty repays close examination.

134

Pulmonària   Lungwort   *Boraginaceae*   Borage Family

P. officinàlis (*P. maculàta*) comes from Europe. I find something a bit morbid about the mottled leaves of this plant but the tubular flowers held above them on stems up to 6 to 8 inches high, with pink buds turning to a soft blue, reminiscent of mertensia, are an interesting addition to the Primrose Path where they get the shade and woodland soil they like. It spreads fairly quickly, can be used as a ground cover, and is easily divided.

Ramónda   Ramonda or Ramondia   *Gesneriaceae*
Gesneria Family

R. pyrenàica. The first view of a flowering ramonda is a thrill. It belongs to the same family as the African violet but, instead of being a tender plant, it is definitely perennial here. It is a persistent species, one of the oldest in cultivation, and most beautiful when well grown. It resents too much water on its hairy foliage and its choice is to be planted vertically in light shade under an overhanging rock, or in the crevice between rocks, in peaty soil.

When happy it sends out numbers of potato flowers of lavender with pointed red-gold centers. The clumps of rough leaves multiply and can be divided. Leaf cuttings can be taken. The method is to pull off one or two leaves, being sure to get the small bud or growing point at the bottom of the leaf. The leaf may root without it but will never make a flowering plant. They can also be grown from their dustlike seeds. In this latter manner they came up prolifically and to save them I transplanted them when so tiny that I was accused of losing one under my fingernail. They developed very slowly but some

135

have now been with me for years—only because of their inherently tough constitution, I'm sure.

Rùta Rue   *Rutaceae*   Rue Family

   R. gravèolens (R. officinàlis). Too bad one cannot draw a smell, for the odor of rue is even more characteristic and odd than its greeny-yellow flowers and bluish compound leaves.

It comes from southern Europe but is entirely hardy here, making a 2-foot shrub and seeding around in gravelly soil. It is one of the old herbs supposed to have medicinal qualities. Winter may kill back some of the branches but a good shearing in spring starts it off again.

Sálvia Sage   *Labiatae*   Mint Family

   S. jurisíci, from Serbia, is a low, almost prostrate plant with gray, dissected leaves and soft lavender-blue flowers in summer.

   S. officinàlis, from the Mediterranean regions, is the sage that is used for seasoning. I don't happen to like it for that but I wouldn't be without it in the garden. It makes a 2-foot shrub of dull-finished, pebbly-surfaced, gray-green leaves, sage green to be exact, just covered with spikes of purple flowers in June.

136

It seeds around in this gravelly soil but is easy to control. A heavy shearing after blooming keeps the shrub shapely. There is also a dwarf form.

Sanguinària Bloodroot *Papaveraceae* Poppy Family
 S. canadénsis. We can't do without the pure white flowers of the bloodroot in early spring. Though native woodland plants, they have no objection to growing anywhere in half shade. The number of petals on the flowers vary. They may

be single, semidouble, or fully double. They take on pinkish tones as they fade. The petals drop quickly but, if the plant is allowed to grow into a big clump, it will gladden your spirits for days as new flowers open.

Saponària Soapwort   *Caryophyllaceae* Pink Family

S. *caespitòsa* comes from the Pyrenees. It makes small tufts of narrow leaves and sends up 4-inch stems of deep pink flowers. It should be given a choice position in the sun.

S. *ocymoìdes,* from Europe, makes great mats of leafy stems and covers them with sheets of small pink flowers with purple calyxes, for a long time in late spring. There is a variety

rùbra that has deeper pink flowers, rounder leaves, and does not grow so lustily, nor is it as reliably permanent, though it is striking while it lasts. Where suited, *ocymoides* seeds around and, while young, the seedlings are easy to move. The plant does not have a fibrous root system and its long wandering roots, which dote on getting under big rocks, are sometimes difficult to transplant once it is mature.

Saxìfraga Saxifrage   *Saxifragaceae* Saxifrage Family

Although this is one of the important groups in a large family, surprisingly few gardeners in this country seem to grow them. There are quantities of them, differing greatly, and all hardy. The ones usually grown in gardens can be divided into the encrusted, the *kábschias,* the mossies, and the woodland species. They all do best in partial shade. They have a wide distribution, mostly in mountains.

The encrusted saxifrages, known as *euaizòons,* are rosettes

138

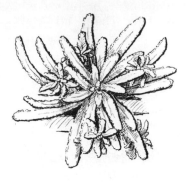

that have white, slightly raised edges to their firm, rather fleshy leaves. Looked at closely, it can be seen that this is a scalloping or toothing, each scallop with a limy deposit on it. The rosettes can be anywhere in size from a dime to a dinner plate, the shapes of the leaves and the length of the flowering stem varying greatly. They all increase their rosettes by offsets. Their airy sprays of flowers can be white, pink, purple, or yellow, and sometimes dotted with a contrasting color. The mere botanical description, however, comes nowhere near telling of their value in our gardens. They are at home among stones, as their name implies, and on or in a wall or ledge of stone they enhance the garden winter and summer. They are, indeed, one of the most attractive plants we can grow for winter use. Their encrustation and their unique beauty can best be appreciated when no flowering plants compete.

Kábschias are considered the queens of the family. Some of them are encrusted too, they make tiny rosettes, each leaf is outlined with lime, and the whole clump looks as though it were exquisitely carved. They form tighter clumps than the *euaizoons*. There is, too, among the *kabschias* a group that have short, stiff linear leaves forming a mat. These bear the largest individual flowers. S. *burseriàna* is typical of this group. These large-flowered *kabschias* do not come up from seed as readily as the rest of the saxifrages.

The mossy saxifrages all have small green leaves, usually in a staghorn pattern. They may be small rosettes that increase rapidly in number, or they may make big leafy mats. The flowers are white, pink, red, yellow, or dotted. The one pic-

139

tured is named Marshal Joffre. It has warm pink flowers and is a little beauty.

S. *umbròsa* or London Pride is the woodland or back-yard type. Its variety *primuloìdes* is a daintier plant than the one that is usually grown. Its scalloped, glossy, evergreen leaves make rosettes 2 to 3 inches wide and send up sprays of

delicate pink flowers from 4 to 8 inches high. The rosettes multiply rapidly in good soil and can be separated and replanted. It has great attraction.

All except some of the *kabschias* come readily from seed. The encrusted sorts divide easily and can be grown as cuttings until they have formed roots. The *kabschias* need careful division because of their tight habit. With care, they can be grown from cuttings.

140

Scabiòsa Mourning Bride   *Dipsaceae* Teasel Family

S. alpìna doesn't look like a mountain flower with its hearty rosette of leaves. However, it is well worth having for

its lavender flowers, 6 to 8 inches high, which continue most of the summer if not allowed to seed. It is readily divided and reseeds moderately.

S. graminifòlia has a more delicate appearance, though

it seems equally hardy. The narrow leaves are silvery. It blooms in August with clear lavender flowers.

S. lùcida is nearer pink but otherwise much like *alpina*.

Sèdum   Stonecrop   *Crassulaceae*   Crassula Family
This is an enormous clan and the species are much confused. Many have synonyms and many are so closely related that it takes a botanist with a lens to differentiate between them. Verbal descriptions are likely to be baffling. Sedums have a way of changing their manner of growth as they mature and the color of the leaves frequently varies with the seasons.

For gardening purposes we can divide sedums into three groups: the weedy spreaders, the good deciduous kinds, and the choice evergreen species that add much to the garden winter and summer. Any fragment of the first group roots where it falls and these sedums become pests. The following list does not contain a tithe of the available species.

S. àcre, from Europe, is one of the most common. It has very small, bright green leaves forming cylindrical columns, and yellow flowers with a greenish cast—a fault of many yellow sedums. It is uncontrollable, almost flat, but where nothing else grows it will make broad mats. It is also good in a flight of steps, if it has them to itself. It keeps out other weeds.

S. álbum, from many lands, is a larger plant with the same habits. It has cylindrical fleshy leaves and white flowers. All these larger spreaders are good plants to hold dry banks, or cover waste places.

S. ánglicum and what I have as *S. lýdium glaùcum* look like the same plant. They make mats of light green leaves that take on tones of red, and they have small pink to white flowers.

Anglicum comes from Europe, the other from Asia Minor. Evergreen, they spread, but not excessively.

S. cauticolum is one of the good deciduous sedums. It comes from Japan and looks something like the better-known

142

sieboldi but has darker gray leaves, is decumbent instead of upright, and blooms with darker pink flowers two weeks before *sieboldi*. It increases slowly and looks good hanging over a wall. A grand plant that blooms in early fall.

S. *dasyphýllum,* from Europe and Africa, is a choice little evergreen with pearly, almost iridescent bluish blobs of leaves.

It has pretty pink stars that are not as attractive as the foliage. This hugs the ground, spreads slowly, and is welcome anywhere.

S. *ellacombiànum* (S. *selskiànum*), from Japan, has 4 inch high clumps of large lettuce-green leaves and yellow flowers in summer. It reminds one of pachysandra but is lighter colored and deciduous. It spreads fairly fast, so makes a good ground cover, but is not a weed.

S. *èwersi,* from the Himalayas, is another good deciduous one. It blooms in late summer with ruby-red flowers over its pale green, fleshy, rather broad leaves, and grows about 6 inches high.

S. *middendorffiànum* is an interesting evergreen. It comes from Siberia, grows about 3 inches high, and is said to have yellow flowers. Mine have never bloomed. However, it is very

welcome for the fine leaves that turn from green to bronze and then leave bright green rosettes on the ground over winter. It spreads slowly.

✳ **S. *nèvii*** is an American that has rosetted leaves of pale green touched with pink, and white flowers up to 3 inches tall that have three-rayed heads. A slow-growing evergreen of great charm.

s'85 jr. WW

S. oregànum, from the Northwest, is an interesting ever-green with fat globular leaves that take on varying tones of

green, yellow, and red, and blooms in July with yellow flowers on 4-inch stems.

S. pleuricàule is a deciduous beauty from Japan. It has tightly clustered, fleshy gray leaves with overtones of other colors, like so many of the good sedums, and fine red flowers in late summer and fall. It creeps slowly, is only an inch or two high, and is well fitted to hang over a ledge or creep between rocks.

S. pulchéllum is an unusually bright, light green. It has pink three-parted flower clusters measuring up to 4 inches in

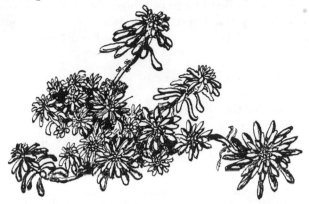

late summer. It is one of our good natives, evergreen, and likes more shade and moisture than most sedums.

S. ròsea (S. rhodìola) comes from the polar regions. In its kitten stage it is a charming little blue-gray bunch of overlapping leaves with an almost bulblike root. As it grows to cat size, 6 to 8 inches, it loses some of its attractiveness and disappointingly produces yellow flowers. It is deciduous.

S. rupéstre is a European. You will notice the accent is on the "pest." It grows a foot high, spreads quickly, and bears yellow flowers in July. It is useful as a ground cover in difficult corners or waste places, but is to be pulled out if it encroaches on better plants.

S. sièboldi, from Japan, is one of the best and best known. Its clumps of 6- to 8-inch-high blue leaves with red edges produce pink flowers in September, just as *cauticolum* goes out of bloom. The clumps increase slowly. It is a good companion for some of the fall gentians and is deciduous, as they are.

S. spathulifòlium is one of our fine western species. The variety I have is *purpùreum*, which is more red than purple but has other colors in the thick-leaved small clusters. It has golden flowers on short stems in summer. It is evergreen at

145

home, but I do not yet know whether it will be truly so here.

S. spùrium is one of the spreaders with its flattish, scalloped leaves. It comes from the Caucasus and has many forms. The one called Dragon's Blood, with reddish leaves and 3-inch-high deep red flowers in late summer, does not ramp as much as some. It is also a good contrast near, but not in, the gentian bed.

Sempervivum   Hen-and-Chickens   *Crassulaceae*
Crassula Family

These, like the sedums, are legion, most of them coming from Europe. They are evergreen and attractive the year round. The rosettes, which increase rapidly by offsets in most species, may be tiny, as in the *arachnoídeum* or cobweb group, or very large, as in *tectòrum*, the common houseleek. The flowers grow on columns of leaves and are fascinating. They may be white, rose, yellow, or purple. The whole column dies after blooming but the other rosettes in the clump carry on. The leaves vary considerably in color. Some are pale to deep green, others may be reddish, purplish, or each leaf may be outlined with a contrasting color. The cobweb species pictured has rich pink flowers.

Sempervivums will grow and bloom in a minimum of soil. They are one of the few plants you can establish on or in a wall that was built with cement or with nothing at all between the stones. A slight depression, a mere whiff of soil, is all they ask. The cracks in large rocks can have a jewellike decoration of sempervivums, given a start of small rooted pieces wedged in and, perhaps, some soil thrown in after them. They are also

146

collectors' items. An area devoted just to sempervivums, show-ing their interesting variety, makes an absorbing study.

Senècio Groundsel   *Compositae* Composite Family
S. *speciòsus* comes from South Africa but is hardy here. It has large rosettes of hairy, toothed leaves, making 6- to 8-inch mats from which spring 12- to 15-inch stems with sprays of purple daisies. The color is a clear amethyst with deeper

purple tones. It is clean and pleasing. It blooms for a long time in early summer and will keep on if the fading blooms are cut. It also makes a good cut flower. A pleasant association in the garden is to plant it near the low geraniums, their colors (from light to dark pinks and reds) toning in beautifully with the *senecio*.

Shórtia Oconee-Bells   *Diapensiaceae* Diapensia Family
S. *galacifòlia.* This is one of our loveliest native plants. It creeps around in peaty, sandy soil in part shade and makes

147

a superior ground cover. The white flowers in early spring are simply exquisite. The glossy leaves, which take on autumn colors, are interesting and most attractive in themselves. The clumps divide readily.

Silène Campion   *Caryophyllaceae* Pink Family

S. acaùlis comes from the high mountains of Europe and America. It makes low clumps of small leaves with small pink flowers close upon them. It has the charm of all the concise mountain plants but actually is not as beautiful as many of its cousins, the small pinks, so that if it proves to be a short-lived perennial, one can accept its performance with equanimity.

S. alpéstris grows about 4 inches high, has chalk-white flowers, and is thoroughly trustworthy and hardy. A very pleasant summer-blooming plant.

S. caroliniàna(S. pennsylvánica) grows 6 to 8 inches high, with 1-inch-wide fine pink flowers, in some forms almost red. It blooms in spring and is very fine indeed. It is usually found growing in light shade in woodland soil.

S. keiskei comes from Japan. It is a small plant with deep pink flowers that bloom in late summer and so has added value. However, I have not found it a very long-lived perennial.

S. marítima islándica is a European. The small gray leaves with touches of red and the big white flowers with their

inflated calyxes make a surprising plant. It is a charming addition to wall or ledge, where its low creeping habit will show to advantage.

S. scháfta, from the Caucasus, grows into 6-inch-high spreading mounds of leafy stems, covered from late summer on with rather small, deep pink flowers. Its greatest value is its late bloom, for the pink of the flowers is sometimes a bit hard, though this varies in different plants.

S. whérryi is very close to *caroliniana* and has lovely, large, warm pink flowers on 6-inch stems.

Sisyrinchium   Blue-eyed-Grass   *Iridaceae*   Iris Family
    S. bráchypus is a very nice yellow "blue-eyed-grass." It comes from California and acted annual with me.
    S. doúglasi (S. grandiflòrum), the queen of the group, has, so far, eluded me. It comes from our western mountains, has gorgeous silky hanging cups in blue or white, and is thoroughly hardy when made to feel at home.
    S. mucronàtum grows 6 to 8 inches high and bears blue flowers. A habit of this *sisyrinchium* is to open only in the afternoon, thus reversing the way of the blue flax, which is open

only in the morning (unless on a cloudy day when the flowers hold longer). Like the others, it is a native American.

Teùcrium   Germander   *Labiatae*   Mint Family
    T. chamaèdrys is a glossy-leaved European shrublet growing a foot high. It is frequently used as a hedge or as edging for a border because it can be trimmed and kept formal if desired. The deep rose-colored flowers open unevenly, contributing color in July when it is most needed, but the main value of the plant is its good foliage. It is practically evergreen, though it may kill partly back in bad winters. In such a case a good shearing in spring will rejuvenate it. It can be divided, grown from seed, or from cuttings taken of half-ripened wood in summer.

150

Thalictrum Meadow-Rue   *Ranunculaceae*
                                   Crowfoot Family

    T. kiusianum, from Japan, is only 3 or 4 inches high but concentrates a lot of charm in that space. It spreads by stolons and will run along the crevice of a rock or make a colony in

partial shade, displaying here its pinkish-lavender fluffy flowers. These are mostly stamens. It is easy to divide.

Thymus Thyme   *Labiatae*   Mint Family
    There are lots of thymes. They may be very flat creepers,

151

may mound up to 3 or 4 inches, or be small shrubs. All are aromatic. They come from many lands.

T. citriodòrus is the celebrated lemon-thyme. It has pale pink flowers and may have silver or gold edges to the tiny leaves. It is a creeping shrubby plant 6 to 8 inches high. Since it will live through all but the worst winters, it is advisable to give it a warm, sheltered position. It divides readily.

T. serpýllum is mother-of-thyme and has many children. They all make mats, spreading by rooting stems, and most of them creep fast and far, so that they must not be placed where they can smother other plants. Variety *álbus* is a slow creeper, one of the very flattest. It has tiny leaves and snowy white flowers, making it very effective and safe to place in good company. *Coccíneus* is a bit larger, though still very flat, and has crimson flowers, small leaves, and is one of the best for between stepping stones. All can stand a bit of walking on. *Lanuginòsus* is a woolly one with lavender flowers, very pretty but not quite as easy to get started. Still, it is hardy when established.

The true *serpýllum* type has pinkish to purplish flowers and makes thick mats that ramp and cover big areas. It is used for thyme lawns in England and would do the job here, too, keeping out grass and weeds.

T. vulgàris, the common thyme, the one used for seasoning, blooms earlier than the others (they are mostly summer-blooming). It has lavender flowers and minute leaves on shrubs up to 8 inches high. It is winter hardy but develops very slowly from seed.

Tiarélla Foam-Flower *Saxifragaceae* Saxifrage Family

T. whérryi is a grand plant for half shade, making clumps of good foliage that have creamy, apricot-tipped flowers in late spring. They keep on blooming for a long time and then the leaves take up the color, showing warm autumn tints. It is close to *T. cordifòlia* but does not spread by stolons as that one does and has more deeply lobed and cut leaves. It can be grown from seed or division.

152

Townséndia   Townsendia   *Compositae*

Composite Family

T. exscàpa (*T. serícea, wilcoxiàna*). All the townsendias are western natives. They are all lovely daisies. *Exscapa* makes small mounds of narrow gray leaves almost completely hidden

from view in spring by the large flowers that may be lavender, pink, or white. It needs especially good drainage in gravelly soil.

T. párryi is a slightly taller plant with sage-green leaves and 8-inch-high lavender daisies.

T. rothrócki is another of the cushion type, with smaller foliage but otherwise like *parryi*, and with lavender daisies close upon it.

All these are choice plants for forward positions in sun or light shade, but they must have good drainage, though they appreciate moisture in their growing season.

Tradescántia   Spiderwort   *Commelinaceae*

Spiderwort Family

T. bracteàta. I mention this only as a warning. This dwarf spiderwort grows about a foot high and has the usual narrow, folded leaves. It blooms in late spring with lovely flowers in

153

pink, blue, purple, or white. It spreads, however, unmercifully, and once it gets roothold is very difficult to eradicate. Any bit of root left in the ground seems to have the ability to make a new plant. It also seeds around and comes up in the middle of more precious plants. Its main value is in waste or moist places where nothing else grows well except weeds and there it will occupy the ground and provide color.

Tróllius Globe-Flower *Ranunculaceae*

Crowfoot Family

    T. europaèus is a superb plant for a moist location, with its fine, large, glossy, deeply cut leaves in 8-inch clumps. Its ball-like blooms of gold or orange are held well above the foliage. It flowers in late spring and occasionally thereafter.

    T. pùmilus, from the Himalayas, is entirely different. It is not a globe-flower but looks like a large yellow buttercup on its 4-inch stems, topping its clump of small, cut leaves. It

thrives in sun or part shade in moist ground or soil that is kept reasonably wet with the hose. It is spring-blooming and can be divided.

W · **Tùnica** Coat-Flower *Caryophyllaceae* Pink Family

    T. saxífraga comes from the Mediterranean region and makes mats of short grass with wiry stems 6 to 8 inches high, covered with clouds of soft pink or white flowers that bloom for most of the summer and fall. When they begin to get a bit seedy looking, a trimming back starts them all over again. There is a double form with tiny, deep pink "roses." It has a more reclining habit and is also a nonstop bloomer all summer.

154

Both like poor soil in sun but are hardy and indestructible. In fact, one has to watch that the single form does not seed around excessively.

Verbèna Verbena *Verbenaceae* Verbena Family
  V. *bipinnatifida*, from our West, is a hardy perennial, a slow creeper that carries heads of flowers of a pleasing pinkish-

purple tone. It blooms in July when color is at a premium. Its small mats can be divided.

Verónica Speedwell *Scrophulariaceae* Figwort Family
  In addition to the tall border species there are ever so many low species, including many creepers, all of which divide readily.
  V. *armèna* not only heads the list but is usually the first to flower in spring. Its furry mats of very fine leaves have large,

very blue flowers close upon them. It must have a well-drained location because the leaves can't stand being waterlogged, but it has a strong constitution; even if hurt, it usually revives.

V. filifórmis, naturalized from Asia Minor, is considered a weed by most people. It is often found growing in lawns. It is, however, a species of many uses. Almost evergreen, it makes big, flat mats and is fine between stepping stones. It also makes an excellent ground cover. I like to use it in association with such plants as small primroses—*farinosa,* for instance—that like root company and can compete successfully with this veronica. It has brilliant blue and white flowers in spring. These surprise you with their sudden appearance some morning. If it takes over too enthusiastically, it is not difficult to pull out.

V. frùticans (V. saxátilis) is a European. It is a 6-inch, glossy-leaved evergreen shrublet with blue flowers and a white eye rimmed in red. It is much prettier than it sounds. Unfortunately, its lovely flowers are fleeting. The foliage may be partly winterkilled; a warm, protected position is advisable.

V. fruticulòsa, from southern Europe, is also a shrubby evergreen, but its pale pink flowers are disappointing.

V. gentianoìdes, also European, takes its name from its

basal rosette of leaves that reminds one of *Gentiana decumbens*. The spikes of very pale blue flowers are not showy until the plants mature. Then the five or six spikes of flowers from 4 to 10 inches high make a pleasing mass of soft color, a fine foil for more highly colored flowers. It is easily divided.

V. incàna, from Russia, has light gray leaves with 8-inch spikes of purple flowers. It has long been used in gardens, not surprisingly, for it is hardy, striking, and has a long season of bloom (like all the spiky veronicas) if the flowers are not allowed to go to seed. It blooms in late spring and divides readily.

V. pectinàta, from Asia Minor, is another very early spring bloomer. Its sage-green, toothed and cut, soft, furry leaves make big mats soon covered with blue flowers. There is a pink variety, much woollier and not so good a plant, as well as a white form. Sections of the rooting mat can be taken off with a spade and replanted. It is excellent as a ground cover along the edge of walks or to hold and clothe low banks.

V. rèpens, from Corsica, is as flat as they come. Its smooth, glossy little leaves root as they run and are garnished by pale blue flowers in spring. It is a perfect ground cover where large mats are wanted and is also good between stepping stones or in a paved terrace.

V. spicàta, from Europe and Asia, has long been used for a medium-height plant in borders but it also has a number of good lower varieties. *Erìca* is 6 to 8 inches high and produces flowers of an attractive pink. It is July-blooming and continues a long time. Variety *nàna* grows only 3 inches high and has little spikes of purplish-blue flowers in summer. Variety *corymbòsa* is a foot high, with pale blue flowers. All can be endlessly divided.

Vìola Violets and violas   *Violaceae* Violet Family

These can be among our most precious plants but they also can be among the worst weeds, though always beautiful. I have grown a number of the high alpines and the western species from seed and will continue to do so, but they have never stayed with me long. The bedding violas, in lovely and widely varied colors, are hybrids and not really hardy here,

157

though some might live over a winter. If you have time and energy to grow them they fill the garden with color over a long period in spring and summer. Aside from a number of local violets that come up all over the place, the only permanent ones I have are the following:

V. arenària ròsea, native to this country and Europe, has small, deep pink flowers among small leaves. It seeds around but is not a nuisance.

V. elàtior, from Europe, has an almost vinelike habit, grows to 18 inches tall, and has large, soft blue flowers with a furry white eye on 2-inch stalks in the angles of the leaves along most of the stem. It must be grown in sun to show its flowers, for in shade it considers the closed or self-fertilizing cleistogamous flowers all that is necessary.

V. odoràta comes from many lands. It is most variable, both as to size and color. There are many hybrids, including large double ones in named varieties. Mine are small purple ones that grow in shade, bloom very early, and surprise you some warm sunny morning in early spring by bursting into bloom and filling the air with sweetness.

V. pedàta, the birdsfoot violet, is a native and one of the loveliest. The type is the two-toned one shown, with velvet purple upper petals, lavender lower ones, and eye of gold.

The leaves enlarge as the flowers fade. Variety *linearíloba* is solidly lavender and there is also a white form. *Pedata* is usually found growing on dry banks in sun or partial shade. A sandy soil suits it but it will also grow prolifically along railroad embankments and other such unlikely places, indicating that its need is for good drainage above all.

158

V. *priceàna* is the Confederate violet, with large leaves and large white flowers heavily lined with blue. It is beautiful, but beware! One plant will populate your entire garden in no time at all and you will spend the rest of your life weeding it out of especially choice plants.

V. *rugulòsa*, another native, is tall and leafy with white flowers. Contained in a tight spot it hasn't become a nuisance.

V. *striàta*, also a native, is creamy white and a good one. It stays put pretty well in sun but goes on the rampage in the shade.

V. *trícolor* is one of the parents of the Johnny-jump-ups that brighten our gardens all season and will even open an eye or two on mild days in winter. Who would want to do without them? There is Bowles Black, black velvet with an eye of gold, and there are endless combinations of colors and great variation in size. Some are almost as big as pansies, while others are real miniatures. They are easy to pull out if they like your garden too much.

Wahlenbérgia, see *Edraianthus.*

LIST OF SUCCESSION OF BLOOM AT CLOUD HILL

This list is, of course, applicable only to climates similar to that of my northeast Pennsylvania region. In colder or warmer parts of the country the months are necessarily different. The seasons vary, too, but except in most unusual ones, the order of bloom remains the same. My list was compiled from notes taken in my garden over a number of years. Some plants mentioned here are not mentioned in the Descriptive List of Plants, but these omissions do not mean that they are not hardy or attractive. For convenience, the following list has been alphabetized.

FEBRUARY
Erica
Viola

MARCH
Draba—very early.
Eranthis—earliest.
Iris reticulata—early.
Primula denticulata—early.
Primula farinosa, frondosa, rosea, vulgaris blue.

APRIL
Androsace sarmentosa

Androsace sempervivoides
Anemone blanda
Antennaria—late.
Aquilegia canadensis, jonesi—late.
Arabis
Dodecatheon—late.
Doronicum—late.
Erigeron—late.
Gentiana verna
Hepatica—early.
Houstonia—late, then on and off all season.
Hutchinsia—late and through May.
Iberis pygmaea, saxatilis
Iris chamaeiris and *pumila* hybrids
Iris pumila atroviolacea—very early.
Omphalodes—late.
Phlox divaricata
Phlox subulata—late.
Polemonium—late.
Potentilla alba—late, then on and off rest of season.
Potentilla eriocarpa—long season.
Potentilla nevadensis
Primula, atrodentata, cachemiriana, clusiana, darialica, denticulata, farinosa, frondosa, juliana, kisoana, polyantha, pubescens, rosea, veris, vulgaris—all continue into May.
Pulmonaria—late.
Sanguinaria—early.
Townsendia
Viola arenaria rosea—on and off all season.
Viola odorata—very early.
Viola pedata—reblooms in fall.
Viola priceana and many others

MAY
Achillea—continues into June.
Actinea

Aethionema
Aethionema warleyensis—early.
Ajuga
Alyssum idaeum
Alyssum saxatilis—early.
Androsace sarmentosa, spinulifera, villosa
Anemone narcissiflora, sylvestris
Aquilegia akitensis—early.
Aquilegia clematiflora, ecalcarata
Aquilegia flabellata—early.
Aquilegia pyrenaica—late.
Aquilegia scopulorum
Aquilegia viridiflora—early.
Arenaria montana—late.
Arenaria laricifolia, verna caespitosa
Armeria juniperifolia—early.
Armeria maritima laucheana
Asperula
Aster alpinus, farreri—late.
Aubrieta
Bellis rotundifolia—early and on and off all season.
Brunnera—early.
Cerastium—late.
Chrysogonum—late and on and off all season.
Coreopsis—long season.
Convallaria—late.
Corydalis
Delphinium bicolor, tatsienense
Dianthus arenaria—late.
Dianthus deltoides—late and into June.
Dianthus nitidus—very early.
Dianthus alpinus, glacialis, gratianopolitanus—the last into June.
Dicentra—into June and on.
Dodecatheon
Draba sibirica—early.

163

Dracocephalum nutans

Epimedium—late, white form latest.

Erinus—late.

Gentiana acaulis group

Geranium alpinum, cinereum, farreri, grandiflorum, macror-rhizum—all into June.

Geranium renardi

Geranium sanguineum hybrids, including *lancastriense*—continue on and off all season.

Globularia

Gypsophila cerastoides—late.

Helianthemum—late.

Heuchera—late and on most of summer.

Hieracium—late and into June.

Iberis gibraltarica, semperflorens, sempervirens—the last has long season.

Iris arenaria, bloudowi, flavissima—early.

Iris cristata, douglasiana, and other western Iris

Iris gracilipes, graminea, sintenisi—late.

Iris tectorum (white form comes first), *verna*

Lewisia cotyledon hybrids, *rediviva*

Linaria alpina and hybrids—late, till frost.

Linum alpinum—early.

Linum perenne—long season.

Lychnis

Mazus

Mertensia—early.

Myosotis scorpioides—late, and rest of season.

Myositis sylvatica (alpestris)—early, long season.

Papaver rupifragum—late, continuing on and off.

Penstemon digitalis, hirsutus—late.

Phlox nivalis, procumbens, stolonifera

Physaria—early.

Polemonium reptans

Potentilla ambigua

Potentilla argyrophylla—late, continuing into June.

164

Potentilla fruticosa forms and hybrids—continue all summer.
Potentilla rupestris and *nana, verna*
Primula auricula—early.
Primula candelabra—start in May continue into June (Japanese earliest).
Primula carniolica, chionantha
Primula chrysopa (gemmifera)—late.
Primula cortusoides—and into June.
Primula elatior
Primula heucherifolia, involucrata, yargongensis
Primula nivalis
Primula polyneura—late.
Primula pulverulenta—late and into June.
Primula saxatilis, secundiflora, sieboldi, viscosa
Ramonda—on into June.
Saponaria
Saxifraga (encrusted), *kabschia*
Scabiosa alpina—on and off all season.
Sedum nevi, rosea
Shortia
Silene acaulis, alpestris—late.
Silene maritima islandica
Silene wherryi—and into June.
Sisyrinchium
Tiarella—early, long season.
Tradescantia—late.
Trollius—late.
Veronica armena, gentianoides, pectinata, repens—early.
Veronica filiformis, fruticans, fruticulosa
Viola elatior, rugulosa, striata, and others

JUNE
Alyssum alpestre, argenteum
Androsace lanuginosa
Anemone canadensis
Armeria plantaginea

Aster purdyi, forresti
Astilbe hybrids—late.
Callirhoe—and till frost.
Campanula collina, elatines, garganica, persicifolia, planiflora, poscharskyana—the last two on and off all season.
Campanula rotundifolia—and till frost.
Corydalis
Crassula
Cyclamen coum hybrids
Delphinium belladonna and *bellamosum, nudicaule*
Dianthus barbatus, neglectus, and many hybrids and other species.
Digitalis
Dracocephalum grandiflorum
Edraianthus
Gentiana bisetaea, cruciata, freyniana
Gentiana septemfida—long season.
Geranium robertianum—long season, till frost.
Geranium wallichianum—late, till frost.
Gypsophila fratensis, repens—long season.
Hippocrepis
Hypericum
Iris chrysographes, Dutch, *forresti*
Jasione—and on.
Lavandula
Leontopodium
Mitchella
Oenothera fremonti—and all season.
Penstemon johnsonae and others
Phyteuma
Potentilla nepalensis—long season.
Potentilla tormentillo, tridentata—on and off all season.
Primula candelabra, florindae, mooreana, sikkimensis
Ruta
Salvia jurisici, officinalis
Saxifraga mossy, *umbrosa*—early.

Scabiosa graminifolia—late and on.
Sedum acre, dasyphyllum, ellacombianum
Sempervivum
Senecio
Silene caroliniana
Thalictrum—late.
Thymus citriodorum
Tunica—on till frost.
Veronica spicata erica, incana, nana—long season.

JULY
Asclepias
Astilbe simplicifolia
Bellium minutum
Calceolaria
Calluna—and on.
Campanula carpatica and *turbinata, cochlearifolia, glomerata acaulis*
Celsia
Cymbalaria muralis—and on till frost.
Dianthus noeanus
Erodium manescavi—on till frost.
Gentiana asclepiadea, calycosa, decumbens, gracilipes
Gentiana hexa-farreri—and on.
Gentiana saponaria
Hypoxis—and on.
Linum flavum
Lotus corniculatus
Potentilla fragiformis
Primula luteola
Pterocephalus
Sedum album, oreganum, rupestre, spurium
Silene schafta—late and on.
Teucrium
Thymus serpyllum
Verbena bipinnatifida

167

AUGUST
Anemone hupehensis
Aster kumleini
Aster low hybrids—late.
Astilbe chinensis pumila—long season.
Ceratostigma
Cyclamen europaeum, neapolitanum—and on.
Gentiana inverleith, ornata, sino-ornata, veitchiorum and many hybrids—most continue till frost.
Sedum pulchellum, spathulifolium
Second bloom of many early flowers that were cut back, such as *coreopsis, dianthus.*

SEPTEMBER
Anemone japonica
Chrysopsis
Gentiana andrewsi, farreri, scabra buergeri—some till frost.
Sedum cauticolum—early.
Sedum pleuricaule, sieboldi
Silene keiskei

October still has color from single chrysanthemums and all the other flowers that bloom till frost: *Campanula rotundifolia,* etc.

BIBLIOGRAPHY

The following list includes only those books which have been most helpful to me:

Berry, G. H., *Gentians in the Garden*. New York, Farrar, Straus & Young, Inc., 1951.

Corsar, K. C., *Primulas in the Garden*. London, Lindsay Drummond.

Cox, E. H. M. and Taylor, G. C., *Primulas for Garden and Greenhouse*. London, Dulau & Co., 1928.

Farrer, Reginald, *The English Rock Garden*. London, T. C. & E. C. Jack, Ltd., 1925.

Gabrielson, Ira N., *Western American Alpines*. New York, Macmillan, 1932.

Jekyll, Gertrude, *Wall and Water Gardens*. New York, Charles Scribner's Sons, 1920.

Wilder, Louise Beebe, *My Garden and Rock Garden*. New York, Doubleday, Page & Co.

Wilkie, David, *Gentians*. New York, Charles Scribner's Sons, 1936.

SEED NURSERIES

The following are the nurseries with which I have dealt most frequently and found to be thoroughly reliable:

Alpenglow Gardens
   13328 Trans-Canada Highway
   New Westminster, British Columbia
   Canada

Claude A. Barr (for native Midwest seeds)
   Prairie Gem Ranch
   Smithwick, South Dakota

Stuart Boothman
   Nightingale Nursery
   Maidenhead, England

Barnhaven Gardens (primroses)
   Gresham, Oregon

Jack Drake
   Inshriach Alpine Plant Nursery
   Aviemore, Inverness-shire
   Scotland

Frank Rose (for native Midwest seeds)
   Missoula, Montana

170

INDEX OF COMMON NAMES

171

172

NOTES

NOTES

NOTES

NOTES

NOTES

NOTES